Air Protection in the European Union Member States

Member states of the European Union often label themselves as the world's top Green Leaders. *Air Protection in the European Union Member States* examines the EU members' air protection policies by taking into consideration wider political, social, and economic perspectives.

The book is divided into four chapters, each focusing on different aspects of the European Union's environmental policies and the member states' air protection efforts: "Green and Smart – The Development of the European Union's Environmental Policies", "Ever Cleaner Union and the Air Protection Concept", "Trends of Air Pollution in the European Union – Comparative Perspective", and "In-Depth Case Studies". These chapters provide a comparative approach to emerging emission trends within the European Union, paying particular attention to key events spanning 2020–2023, such as the implementation of the Green Deal, the reinterpretation of the meaning of public health caused by the COVID-19 pandemic, and the strategic withdrawal from hydrocarbons accelerated by the outbreak of war in Ukraine. Throughout the book, three main categories of states are characterized: leaders, second-raters, and laggards.

Air Protection in the European Union Member States presents a combination of general discussions, legislative analyses, comparative studies, and detailed case studies, demonstrating the origin, development, and trends in air protection policies within the European Union. This uniquely interdisciplinary book will be a vital guide for students, researchers, and teachers in the fields of global studies, international relations, and political and economic science.

Magdalena Tomala is an associate professor in the Department of Management and Computer Modelling, Kielce University of Technology, Poland. She conducts research on governance in public policies and international relations. Her main areas of research are issues of economy, sustainable development, ecology, and international cooperation. She is the author of the monographs *Greenland, in the System of International Relations in the Light of Immanuel Wallerstein's Systems-Worlds Theory* (2016) and *Sustainable Development of the Baltic Sea Region* (2020); she has co-authored *The Northern Dimension of the European Union. Political and Legal Study* (2009), *Politics and Development in the North American Arctic* (2021), and *Public Policy and the Impact of COVID-19 in Europe* (2022).

Katarzyna Dośpiał-Borysiak is an associate professor at the University of Lodz (Poland), Faculty of International and Political Studies. She specializes in sustainable development, climate policies, and regionalism. Her main geographical scope for research is the European Union, especially Nordic countries and Poland. She is the author of three books covering various regional perspectives – for example, *Civic and Uncivic Values in Poland: Value Transformation, Education, and Culture* (2019, co-edited with Sabrina Ramet and Kristen Ringdal) – and over 50 scientific articles, chapters, and reviews.

Routledge Insights in Tourism Series
Series Editor: Anukrati Sharma
Head & Associate Professor of the Department of Commerce and Management at the University of Kota, India

This series provides a forum for cutting edge insights into the latest developments in tourism research. It offers high quality monographs and edited collections that develop tourism analysis at both theoretical and empirical levels.

Tourism and Poverty Alleviation in Nature Conservation Areas
A Comparative Study Between Japan and Vietnam
Nguyen Van Hoang

Sport Tourism, Events and Sustainable Development Goals
An Emerging Foundation
Edited by Anukrati Sharma, Miha Lesjak and Dusan Borovcanin

Tourism, Philanthropy and School Tours in Zimbabwe
Problematising "Win-Win" Discourses
Kathleen Smithers

Metaverse and Tourism
Rethinking Implications on Virtual Reality
Edited by Marco Valeri and Ahmad Albattat

Developing the Frontiers of Casino Tourism
Progress and Prospects in East and Southeast Asia
Ricardo C.S. Siu

Air Protection in the European Union Member States
From Pushers to Laggards
Magdalena Tomala and Katarzyna Dośpiał-Borysiak

For more information about this series, please visit: www.routledge.com/Routledge-Insights-in-Tourism-Series/book-series/RITS

Air Protection in the European Union Member States

From Laggards to Pushers

Magdalena Tomala and Katarzyna Dośpiał-Borysiak

Routledge
Taylor & Francis Group

LONDON AND NEW YORK

First published 2025
by Routledge
4 Park Square, Milton Park, Abingdon, Oxon OX14 4RN

and by Routledge
605 Third Avenue, New York, NY 10158

Routledge is an imprint of the Taylor & Francis Group, an informa business

© 2025 Magdalena Tomala and Katarzyna Dośpiał-Borysiak

British Library Cataloguing-in-Publication Data
A catalogue record for this book is available from the British Library

Library of Congress Cataloging-in-Publication Data
Names: Tomala, Magdalena, author. | Dośpiał-Borysiak, Katarzyna, 1976– author.
Title: Air protection in the European Union member states : from laggards to pushers / Magdalena Tomala, Katarzyna Dośpiał-Borysiak.
Description: Abingdon, Oxon ; New York, NY : Routledge, 2025. | Includes bibliographical references and index.
Identifiers: LCCN 2024027360 (print) | LCCN 2024027361 (ebook) | ISBN 9781032706986 (hardback) | ISBN 9781032706993 (paperback) | ISBN 9781032707006 (ebook)
Subjects: LCSH: Air—Pollution—Government policy—European Union countries. | Air quality management—European Union countries.
Classification: LCC HC240.9.A4 T66 2025 (print) | LCC HC240.9.A4 (ebook) | DDC 363.738094—dc23/eng/20240805
LC record available at https://lccn.loc.gov/2024027360
LC ebook record available at https://lccn.loc.gov/2024027361

ISBN: 978-1-032-70698-6 (hbk)
ISBN: 978-1-032-70699-3 (pbk)
ISBN: 978-1-032-70700-6 (ebk)

DOI: 10.4324/9781032707006

Typeset in Times New Roman
by Apex CoVantage, LLC

Contents

Figures

Tables

Introduction

Katarzyna Dośpiał-Borysiak

Albert Einstein once said, "We cannot solve our problems with the same thinking we used when we created them". It perfectly reflects attitudes toward the world's environmental challenges in the 21st century. The harm has already been done, but the solutions are waiting, and they must be applied, shared, and embraced by countries and societies. Unlike other ecological threats that became highly visible in the last decades of the 20th century, such as climate change or ocean acidification, air pollution has been known since ancient times. As indicated by Fowler et al. (2020) Hippocrates demonstrated the relationship between air and health in his book from about 400 BCE titled *Airs, Waters,* and *Places*; the first act on air pollution, "the Smoke Abatement Act", dates back to 1273 and prohibits the use of coal for health reasons and in 1872, Robert Angus Smith published *Air and Rain: The Beginnings of a Chemical Climatology* presenting the results of multipollutant measurements.

The simplest definition of air pollution (AP) would refer to the presence of harmful or excessive substances in the air, such as gases, particles, and chemicals, which can pose risks to human health, the environment, and the climate. In the understanding of the European Union's Ambient Air Quality Directives, there are 13 main air pollutants: sulphur dioxide (SO_2), nitrogen dioxide (NO_2) and nitrogen oxides (NO_x), particulate matter (PM_{10}, $PM_{2.5}$), ozone (O_3), benzene, lead, carbon monoxide (CO), arsenic, cadmium, nickel, and benzo(a)pyrene.

Their impact on human health is extensive. According to the World Health Organization (WHO) (2024), air pollution is one of the most dangerous causes of non-communicable diseases, ranking just below hypertension, tobacco smoking, and high glucose as one of the main causes of death. There are annually an estimated 7 million premature deaths globally attributed to air pollution, making it one of the major environmental causes of death. Lung diseases and lung cancer are the next most common causes of premature deaths linked to air pollution, followed by heart disease and stroke. In addition, both brief and prolonged exposure to air pollution can worsen asthma, cause respiratory infections, and impair lung function. It also has negative effects on fertility, pregnancy, new-borns, and children. Additionally, there is growing evidence

DOI: 10.4324/9781032707006-1

linking air pollution exposure to obesity, systemic inflammation, dementia, Alzheimer's disease, and new-onset type 2 diabetes in adults. Most vulnerable groups, such as children, pregnant women, and the elderly, appear to be particularly affected in low- and middle-income countries. These significant global health costs, which account for 6.1% of the world's gross domestic product (more than US$8 trillion), also pose a significant threat to the public health economy, according to the World Bank (2022).

Apart from its negative effects on human health, air pollution poses a threat to the environment due to its contribution to acidification, eutrophication, and ozone depletion, which can harm crops, forests, and ecosystems. For example, eutrophication, a result of nitrogen deposition, surpasses critical loads in two-thirds of ecosystem areas in the European Union (EU), significantly impacting biodiversity. Additionally, by aggravating nitrogen surpluses through water pollution, this pollution pressure further jeopardizes sustainability and environmental integrity. Additionally, some pollutants, like black carbon (BC), a component of PM, are short-lived climate forcers that directly contribute to global warming.

The air pollution problem also has regional variations. Asia, primarily countries like China, India, and Nepal, but also Africa and the Middle East, is witnessing the most alarming trends. Europe is also affected by a high level of industrialization and urbanization. The difference between pollution in large metropolises and rural areas is equally appealing. In the case of the latter, it is pollution from traffic, industry, and construction, and the latter is caused mainly by indoor air pollution from biomass burning for cooking and heating.

The question remains whether the international community reflected these challenges in a proportionate manner, taking into consideration all possible health and economic costs. The roots of global air protection regulations can be traced back to the mid-20th century when industrial activities and the burning of fossil fuels began significantly impacting air quality. The infamous London smog of 1952, which resulted in thousands of deaths, served as a wake-up call, prompting nations to initiate collaborative efforts. The first major international agreement addressing transboundary air pollution was the 1979 Geneva Convention on Long-Range Transboundary Air Pollution. This marked the beginning of a series of protocols and amendments designed to reduce emissions of sulphur dioxide, nitrogen oxides, and other pollutants. Since the 1990s, there has been a recognized interconnection between air pollution and climate change, as the primary pollutants implicated in air pollution also influence climate dynamics, with many stemming from the same sources as greenhouse gases. In 1992, the United Nations Framework Convention on Climate Change (UNFCCC) provided a broader framework for addressing both climate change and air quality issues. It was however the Kyoto Protocol of 1997, though primarily focused on greenhouse gas emissions, played a crucial role in raising awareness about the interconnectedness of air quality and climate change. Subsequently, the 2015 Paris Agreement further strengthened the commitment to reducing emissions, emphasizing the importance of collective action. Still, despite international efforts in 2019, nearly all of the global population resided in areas where the WHO's most stringent air quality guidelines undertaken in 2021 were not achieved.

The European Union, trying to become the green leader, also introduced extensive policies to combat air pollution. In the first two decades of the 21st century, the main pollutants were reduced by between 13% and 84%, depending on the source. The European Environment Agency (EEA) (2023) estimated that exposure to $PM_{2.5}$ caused about 238,000 premature deaths in 2021. Nitrogen dioxide caused 49,000 deaths, and ozone caused 24,000. This indicates a significant decline compared to the approximately one million annual premature deaths reported in the early 1990s. Nevertheless, 97% of the urban population was still exposed to $PM_{2.5}$ concentrations above the WHO air quality guideline level of 5 μg/m³. The biggest sources of air pollution in Europe are energy consumption and agriculture, so making these sectors more sustainable is a crucial dimension countries should focus on. Because these sectors are also responsible for greenhouse gas emissions, tackling both air pollution and climate change dilemmas is more than justified. The annual cost to public authorities of air pollution was estimated to amount to €231–853 billion. The new standards introduced by the Green Deal were supposed to cost less than 0.1% of GDP, which was at least 7 times lower than the benefits to the economy and society (European Commission, 2022).

The effectiveness of proactive policies has been proven by the fact that over the decade 2012–2021, external costs caused by air pollution from industry decreased by nearly 35%, with the energy sector contributing 80% to the reduction. This undeniable achievement was a result of the adaptation of new technologies and a shift to renewable energy sources and less polluting fuels (European Environment Agency, 2024). However, only more than 100 industrial facilities, mostly coal power plants, contributed to half of the total damage. Estimates placed the general costs at 2% of the EU's GDP, demonstrating that while the EU is making progress, there is still significant room for improvement (European Environment Agency, 2024).

The book presents a combination of general discussions, legislative analyses, comparative studies, and detailed case studies showing the origin, development, and trends in air protection policies within the European Union. It is divided into four chapters, each focusing on different aspects of the European Union's environmental policies and the member states' air protection efforts. The first chapter, titled "Green and Smart: The Development of the European Union's Environmental Policies", explores the global shift towards sustainability and green policies, seen from the perspective of global and national trends. It then shows the historical development of environmental protection within the EU. We analyse the key players, processes, and tools involved. This chapter also discusses the European Green Deal, which, starting in 2019, guides all EU policies, hoping to make Europe a carbon-neutral continent until

2050. The second chapter provides an overview of international air protection efforts and their evolution. It delivers an insight into the legislative framework governing air quality in the EU and evaluates the Green Deal's targets for emissions reduction and the actions taken to achieve these goals. Additionally, it discusses perceptions and responses to air quality and climate issues, as well as the growing need for a participatory culture. The next chapter conducts a comparative analysis of CO_2 emissions trends across different European countries since 2000. It examines the various measures implemented by EU countries to combat air pollution and reviews the successes and challenges faced in enforcing air quality laws. This chapter also discusses the impact of "Black Swans", unexpected events like the COVID-19 pandemic and the Russian invasion of Ukraine, on air pollution levels and policies. Various case studies of countries are the main focus of the last, fourth chapter. This section highlights the diverse approaches and outcomes of air protection in different EU countries, which we divide into leaders, second-raters, and marauders. It provides valuable insights into effective strategies, best tools, and common pitfalls in light of countries' potential. The book includes a discussion, summarizing the findings, drawing conclusions, and offering recommendations for future policies and actions.

Reference list

European Commission. (2022). *Zero pollution: New rules for healthy air.* Fact sheet. https://ec.europa.eu/commission/presscorner/api/files/attachment/873813/Factsheet%20on%20Air%20Quality_EN.pdf.pdf

European Environment Agency. (2023). *Premature deaths due to exposure to fine particulate matter in Europe. Analyses and data.* https://www.eea.europa.eu/en/analysis/indicators/health-impacts-of-exposure-to

European Environment Agency. (2024). *Costs of industrial pollution from the largest facilities decline in Europe but remain at 2% of EU GDP.* Press release. Retrieved January 25, 2024, from https://www.eea.europa.eu/en/newsroom/news/costs-of-industrial-pollution

Fowler, D., Brimblecombe, P., Burrows, J., Heal, M., Grennfelt, P., Stevenson, D., Jowett, A., Nemitz, E., Coyle, M., Liu, X., Chang, Y., Fuller, G., Sutton, M., Klimont, Z., Unsworth, M., & Vieno, M. (2020). A chronology of global air quality. *Philosophical Transactions. Series A, Mathematical, Physical, and Engineering Sciences, 378*(2183), 20190314.

World Bank. (2022). *The global health cost of PM2.5 air pollution: A case for action beyond 2021.* World Bank Group. https://elibrary.worldbank.org/doi/pdf/10.1596/978-1-4648-1816-5

World Health Organization. (2024). *Air pollution: The invisible health threat.* WHO News Room. Retrieved July 12, 2023, from https://www.who.int/news-room/feature-stories/detail/air-pollution – the-invisible-health-threat

1 Green and smart – the development of the European Union's environmental policies

Katarzyna Dośpiał-Borysiak

1.1 The world goes green

What does it mean to go green? It could involve adopting policies, practices, and behaviours that are environmentally friendly and sustainable. Going green also encompasses making fundamental choices that have a positive impact on the environment. On the individual level, it could equal using local products, recycling materials, and supporting eco-friendly initiatives; on the national level, it could mean phasing out coal use, introducing convenient public transport, or applying high eco-taxes; but on the international level, it is about fighting with ozone depletion, protecting endangered species, and combating irreversible climate changes. Overall, going green is mostly about taking action to protect the planet, with all its variety, richness, and beauty. It means a constant process, not only a definite goal.

The first and most crucial fact to understand the situation of the planet Earth is that the human population has grown from 200,000 *Homo sapiens* in 50,000 BCE to 8 billion in 2022, and it is projected to reach 9.8 billion in 2050 and 11.2 billion in 2100 (United Nations, 2024). The second important fact is that each individual regardless of the time – past, present, or future – has basic needs such as food and shelter. However, over time, the concept of a need expanded to include a rich variety of products, and services, let it be a new car or a summer holiday. In the 20th and 21st centuries, humans mostly became consumer societies, functioning well due to the use of the planet's assets, especially non-renewable resources. Simultaneously, they have reached the point when the coming future is filled with uncertainties concerning the Earth's potential to meet all needs. Our discussion in this chapter will primarily focus on the state of the planet and its boundaries, followed by an examination of the human response and the measures implemented to mitigate these challenges.

In 2009, scientists from the Stockholm Resilience Centre proposed the planetary boundaries concept, defining nine boundaries within which humanity can thrive. In September 2023, scientists finally quantified all these boundaries, revealing that six of them have been exceeded. These include

DOI: 10.4324/9781032707006-2

climate change, biosphere integrity, land-system change, freshwater change, biogeochemical flows, and novel entities. Crossing these boundaries increases the risk of significant environmental changes, which may pose a threat to the stability of social systems. The relatively balanced areas, where boundaries have not been transgressed, include stratospheric depletion and atmospheric aerosol loading, but on the other hand, ocean acidification is about to reach the safe operating space (Richardson et al., 2023).

The simplest explanation of the aforementioned challenges lies in human production and consumption patterns that have persisted, starting from the industrial evolution in the mid-19th century. Chronologically, the development of production processes, from energy-intensive industries to rapid urbanization and global food production, has posed significant challenges to environmental sustainability and social equity, both within and between societies. Processes, which emerged in the mid-20th century such as globalization, scientific and technological developments, and international trade have fuelled rising consumption, leading to resource depletion, waste generation, and pollution of air, water, and soil. The transportation sector, a significant contributor to carbon emissions, the production of electronic gadgets consuming rare earth metals, and the resource-intensive fashion industry, to name just a few, have contributed to environmental pollution not only in developed countries but also in developing and rising economies.

It was the availability of energy that has transformed the course of humanity over the last several decades. The global primary energy consumption in 1900 was 12 TWh, but it has grown by ten times till 2000. In 2022, it reached almost 179 TWh, with the most quantity being produced from fossil fuels, such as oil (53 TWh), coal (45 TWh), and natural gas (39 TWh). The rising trend of energy consumption is going to prevail due to the growing wealth and population of many countries. The average citizen in the most energy-consuming countries like Iceland, Norway, Canada, the United States, and rich nations in the Middle East such as Oman, Saudi Arabia, and Qatar will use 100 times more energy than the one in the poorest countries (Ritchie et al., 2024).

In fact, human-made materials outweigh Earth's entire biomass as was revealed by Elhacham et al. (2020, pp. 442–444). The mass of humans is estimated to be only 0.01%, whereas plants constitute 90% of global biomass, followed by bacteria, fungi, archaea, protists, and animals. Despite extensive agriculture, the total mass of domesticated crops is outweighed by the loss of plants due to deforestation, forest management, and land-use changes. Simultaneously, the total anthropogenic mass, comprising concrete, aggregates, bricks, asphalt, metals, and plastic, has doubled almost every 20 years over the past century. This suggests that each person produces more anthropogenic material weekly than their body weight. There is also an element of global justice that must be elaborated in this respect. The material footprint per capita in high-income countries is ten times that of low-income countries. Surprisingly, the global community cannot solve the problem of regions prone to hunger in many parts of the world, but also each person wastes 120 kilograms of food every year (United Nations, 2023).

The scale and complexity of these problems have prompted the international community to engage in reflection. Early considerations were expressed by scientists, who could empirically observe the consequences of human impact on the well-being of the planet. Already in the middle of the 20th century, researchers increasingly pointed out the problem of rising greenhouse gas (GHG) emissions, which they observed even in distant areas like the Mauna Loa Observatory in Hawaii. The vision of planetary catastrophe caused by nuclear weapons was pictured by Bertrand Russell and Albert Einstein, and several other Nobel Prize winners, in their Manifesto from 1955 (Atomic Heritage Foundation, 2024), calling for peaceful solutions to ongoing conflicts. It was the first time in history that humans realised that they obtained both incredible tools to develop and to destroy the planet.

With the release of *Limits to Growth* by Club of Rome experts (Meadows et al.) in 1972, the concept of sustainable development became widely known. This book is still relevant today even though it was written over 50 years ago. It emphasises the idea that there are natural development constraints on contemporary society, and that mankind must acknowledge these limits to prevent unintended effects and survive. It has been determined that the year 2100 marks a tipping point, beyond which civilization's continued existence will be in danger barring notable behavioural shifts.

This scientific concern was first reflected by policy-makers during the UN Environment Conference held in Stockholm in 1972. It was a pivotal moment as it established several guidelines for managing environmental problems and finding balances between economic expansion, resources, and humankind's place in the universe. In 1973, the global energy crisis visibly revealed the dangerous consequences of hydrocarbon dependency and the potential of political pressure that may be exerted by oil and gas exporters. That same year, the German-born British scientist Schumacher published *Small is Beautiful*, the "praise ode" to low-tech policies, which complemented and expanded the existing production paradigm "bigger is better" (Schumacher, 1973). Ironically, nearly half a century later, the Russian invasion of Ukraine led to a similar energy crisis, mostly in Europe, reaffirming the role of small solutions, like portable energy generators.

The last two decades of the 20th century witnessed a profound reflection on balancing seemingly conflicting economic, social, and environmental interests. It was the UN's 1987 report *Our Common Future*, also known as the Brundtland Commission's report, that formally introduced the concept of "sustainable development". It calls for development that satisfies current wants without endangering the capacity of future generations to satisfy their own (United Nations, 1987, p. 41). The concept is often depicted by a Venn diagram with three "E's" (economy, equality, environment), although sometimes a fourth "E", education, is included. It can also be expressed as profit – people – planet. Sustainable management aims to prevent resource depletion, food insecurity, mass migration, and other negative processes that may threaten well-being. The trajectory of this concept, which is inherently broad and ambiguous, deserves attention. Sustainable development has been incorporated into the constitutions of many countries, with all sectors of the economy, as well as public and private entities, expected to adhere to this overarching principle. Moreover, it has encouraged reflection on axiological terms, such as the concept of intergenerational justice, which invokes wide philosophical contemplation (Hector et al., 2014, pp. 7–28).

First, a broader reflection on the implementation of the SD vision took place during the Rio de Janeiro Earth Summit in 1992 – formally, the United Nations Conference on Environment and Development (UNCED). The summit resulted in the adoption of several important agreements, including the Rio Declaration on Environment and Development, the UNFCCC, and the Convention on Biological Diversity. The summit also adopted "the Agenda 21" (referring to the 21st century), a comprehensive, but informal action plan for sustainable development that should guide international organizations, national governments, and local authorities. Rio also outlined standard principles for sustainable development, including the precautionary principle, the polluter pays principle, and the principle of common but differentiated responsibilities.

In 2000, as an opening of the new century, the Millennium Development Goals (MDGs) were accepted by the United Nations. The MDGs were a group of eight international development objectives that were supposed to be accomplished by the year 2015. They addressed a wide range of issues such as gender equality, poverty, hunger, diseases, maternal health, child mortality, and environmental degradation. According to the Millennium Development Goals Monitor (2015) in some of these areas, the real progress was undeniable like a drop in extreme poverty by more than 50%, or more women's parliamentary representation. Regarding environmental conservation, observable successes are indisputable. Ozone-depleting chemicals have been almost completely eradicated since 1990, which should cause the ozone layer to recover by the middle of the century. Globally, the number of marine and terrestrial protected areas has significantly increased, mostly in the Caribbean and Latin America. Access to improved drinking water sources has also improved, as 2.6 billion people gained access since 1990. 147 nations have met the drinking water target, 95 nations have achieved the sanitation target, and 77 nations have met both. Additionally, more than 2 billion people have access to improved sanitation. Moreover, there has been a reduction in the proportion of urban populations in developing nations living in slums, dropping from 39.4 *to* 29.7% between 2000 and 2014.

As a continuation of MDSs the resolution known as *Transforming Our World: A Sustainable Development Agenda for 2030*, or Agenda 2030, was approved by the UN General Assembly in 2015 (United Nations, 2015). It is focused on five areas of crucial importance, the so-called 5 Ps: people, planet, prosperity, peace, and partnership. It delineates 17 Sustainable Development Goals (SDGs), each with 169 sub-targets. While the SDGs are generally applicable to all nations and can be achieved through cooperation, some of them primarily align with national objectives and challenges. Countries select the most important goals for them to concentrate on by 2030, later integrating them within sectoral policies. According to the Agenda 2030, SDGs are, however, not only introduced by countries but also by every private and public company, institution, association, NGO, and member of society.

One of the most crucial yet complex developments within SDGs was climate change. The growing recognition of the urgent need to address climate change on a global scale began with the establishment of the UNFCCC in 1992 (United Nations, 1992). It laid the groundwork for international cooperation and, what is even more crucial, it referred to the anthropogenic character of climate change. Despite these developments, which should at least cease the voices of all global-warning deniers, it was five years later in Kyoto, that countries adopted the Protocol, setting binding targets for developed countries to reduce their GHG emissions. However, it became evident that a more comprehensive and inclusive agreement was needed as developing countries' climate footprint was intensively growing, with the rising population and consumption. This led to the negotiation and adoption of the Paris Agreement in 2015, which aims to limit global warming to well below 2 degrees Celsius above pre-industrial levels. The evident success of the agreement is introducing climate agendas to national policies to a higher extent than it used to be. The agreement also encouraged countries like Japan, China, and EU members to set carbon neutrality goals and embrace net-zero targets. On the other hand, enforceability may pose a challenge as non-legal obligations may force countries to cut emissions. Despite the continuous process of negotiations occurring annually in the form of the Conference of Parties (COP) of the UNFCCC, some countries are still free-riding, failing to fulfil their commitments or adequately contributing to global efforts.

Definitely, the shift towards sustainability, commonly known as "going green", has impacted every aspect of political, economic, and social life. Environmental protection has received significantly more attention in national politics, and this trend prevails in most countries, albeit with varying degrees of intensity. The importance of the ministries of environment and the creation of new bodies like ministries of climate is evidence of the strengthened role of environmental institutions. Although the support for Green Parties is still comparatively low, with a few notable exceptions like Germany, most parties, including conservative parties, have incorporated green agendas.

In terms of economics, the last 15 years have seen the emergence of concepts related to the "green economy", including "green growth", "circular economy", and "cleaner production methods" (Ossewaarde & Ossewaarde-Lowtoo, 2020). These approaches aim to moderate economic activities, advocating for innovative technologies and consumption patterns that minimise negative environmental impacts. Also, citizens, particularly those in post-materialistic societies in the Inglehartian sense (Inglehart, 1977), have become more informed and engaged. The grassroots initiatives have gained momentum alongside classical, well-established organizations like Greenpeace and the World Wildlife Fund. This heightened awareness has translated into stronger political pressure from voters, both at the national and local levels. Simultaneously, individual behaviours towards sustainability have gained much support. Moreover, the role of research has been increased, with the greater access of high-profile specialists and researchers to decision-making processes. Additionally, professional organizations like the Intergovernmental Panel on Climate Change (IPCC), the World Meteorological Organization (WMO), the European Environment Agency (EEA), and others have played more pivotal roles in shaping policies and public opinion on environmental issues. Finally, the process of media communication has been developed to include more scientific findings, instead of emotional plays. However, despite all these positive processes, it is still not enough to prevent human-induced environmental degradation and to keep the planet lush and green as it used to be.

1.2   Evolution of the environmental protection in the European Union

As discussion in the previous section revealed, the world is trying to be more green but the results are still moderate and unsatisfactory. The European Union (EU) may be considered an exemption as it has emerged as a global leader in environmental protection, driven by a complex interplay of historical, political, and economic factors. The evolution of EU environmental policy can be traced through several key phases, each marked by distinct challenges, achievements, and shifts in approach.

The first phase began with the signing of the Treaty of Rome in 1957. The EU's environmental protection policies of the 1950s and 1960s were comparatively simple, with a narrow understanding of environmental issues and minimal regulatory frameworks. The European countries began a period of almost unrestricted industrial development, aiming at the maximalization of economic output. The initial attempt to acknowledge the significance of the environment for the welfare of the EU population was made with the introduction of the Environment Action Programmes in 1973 (the first of which was in effect from 1973 to 1976), marking the beginning of the second period. The major catalyst for reform was the oil crisis of 1973, which highlighted Europe's vulnerability to external energy shocks and forced European leaders to re-evaluate energy policies and the broader environmental implications of growth. This also mirrored the global trend of stronger environmental consciousness reflected by debates during the 1972 United Nations Conference on the Human Environment in Stockholm and the emergence of environmental NGOs and grass-roots activism.

The first wave of environmental legislation focused primarily on pollution control, targeting air and water quality, and biodiversity. Referring to water treatment (as air pollution is to be discussed later), various Directives regulated surface waters, bathing waters, discharges of hazardous substances in surface waters and groundwater, as well the quality of water intended for human consumption. The Waste Framework Directive (1975) introduced measures to prevent waste generation, promote recycling and recovery, and ensure the safe disposal of waste. Also, the Birds Directive (1979) established a network of Special Protection Areas (SPAs) across EU member states, aiming at conserving wild birds and their habitats. Simultaneously, initial steps were taken to assess the environmental impact of public and private projects (1985). According to Burchell and Lightfoot (2001, p. 36), environmental policy emerged as one of the fastest-growing areas between 1973 and 1985, with the issuance of 120 directives, 27 decisions, and 14 regulations.

The ratification of the Single European Act in 1987, marked the beginning of consolidation and expansion of environmental policies in the European Community. The Act focused on protecting the quality of the environment, safeguarding human health, and providing rational use of natural resources. The new title "Environment" provided the first legal basis for a common environment policy, as it introduced environmental protection as a formal objective of EU policy. Later revisions of the treaties also reinforced the Community's dedication to environmental preservation. First, the Treaty of Maastricht (1993) made the environment one of the official EU policy areas. As it also introduced the co-decision procedure and qualified majority voting in the Council, the general rule, and the legal environmental process, was facilitated. The Treaty of Amsterdam (1999), on the other hand, made environmental protection an integral element of all sectoral policies. The growing emphasis was put on sustainable development and biodiversity conservation in the spirit of the Brundtland's Commission Report (1987) and the Rio Earth Summit in 1992. The new global processes influenced the EU's Fifth Environment Action Programme (1993–2000), which emphasised the integration of environmental concerns into other policy areas and the promotion of sustainable consumption and production patterns. Also, with the growing level of ambition, some of the initial solutions were revised like the Birds Directive supplemented with the Habitat Directive (1992), making up the Natura 2000 network of terrestrial and marine protected areas. New regulations were implemented like urban wastewater or nitrates management. During this time, the EU aimed to establish itself as a unified actor on the international stage. It was proven by its attempts to become an international leader and norm entrepreneur in solving major, global challenges like climate change and ozone depletion.

The 2000s saw the EU expand its membership, with the accession of several Central and Eastern European countries. This was a new period for the EU, dominated by internal integration challenges. Until then, environmental issues had only played a minor role in enlargement negotiations. During the first enlargement in 1973 (Denmark, Ireland, and the UK), environmental protection was only in its initial stages, with very limited legal ramifications. The accession of southern countries, starting with Greece in 1981 and followed by Spain and Portugal in 1986, caused only minor tensions. However, during negotiations over the Single European Act, the most recent members prioritised economic growth through increased investment and trade, while northern member states, particularly Denmark, Germany, and the Netherlands, advocated for more advanced environmental and health norms. The 1995 enlargement brought in countries with a profound environmental record, including Austria, Finland, and Sweden, leaving almost no room for conflict of interest. As indicated by Selin and Vandeveer (2015, p. 323), the situation varied with the 2004 enlargement, which included ten new countries (Cyprus, Czech Republic, Estonia, Hungary, Latvia, Lithuania, Malta, Poland, Slovakia, and Slovenia), and the 2007 enlargement with Bulgaria and Romania. Most of these countries share a post-Communist history of environmental degradation, including industrial pollution, deforestation, and inadequate waste management systems. The transition to market economies also strained environmental efforts due to limited resources, weak regulatory frameworks, and competing economic priorities. The EU's Sixth Environment Action Programme (2002–2012) reflected these advancements, focusing on environmental health, and the integration of environmental considerations into economic policies. The program also highlighted the EU's growing commitment to international environmental cooperation, with an emphasis on multilateralism and global partnerships.

Despite the strains of enlargement, the EU's environmental legislation became more comprehensive and ambitious during this period. The Treaty of Lisbon (European Union, 2007), consolidating old and new colliding interests, granted the EU legal personality, allowing it to conclude international agreements. Also, environmental issues fell under shared competencies, and ordinary legislative procedures for environmental policy-making between the Council and the Parliament were established. Moreover, "Combating climate change" became a specific goal, as did sustainable development in relations with third countries. According to Benson and Jordan (2010, p. 469), environmental policy has become more supranational as the level of competence of the member states diminished in areas like civil protection, climate change, energy production, and consumption. In many areas, ambitious solutions complemented these legal frameworks. These included the Water Framework Directive (2000), the Energy Performance of Buildings Directive (2002), the EU Emissions Trading System (EU ETS) in 2005, the REACH Regulation (Registration, Evaluation, Authorization, and Restriction of Chemicals, 2006), the Renewable Energy Directive (2009), and the Industrial Emissions Directive (2010), to name just a few.

The 2010s were characterised by a deeper integration of environmental considerations into all policy areas, reflecting the EU's commitment to mainstreaming sustainability across its internal and external actions. The EU's

Seventh Environment Action Programme (2014–2020) prioritised natural capital, a competitive and low-carbon economy, human health and well-being, law enforcement, knowledge, investment in environmental and climate policy, sustainable cities, and international efforts (European Parliament, Council of the European Union, 2013). Despite high expectations, the 7th EAP's evaluation indicated that implementation could have been better monitored and that environmental spending in Europe remained low over many years (approximately 2% of GDP) (European Commission, 2019). The most important external determinant of the EU's environmental actions was the Paris Agreement in 2015, reinforcing the EU's climate commitments. The parties to the agreement decided to limit the increase in global average temperature to well under 2 degrees Celsius above pre-industrial levels, preferably 1.5 degrees Celsius.

As the paradigm shift was pending, the EU announced in December 2019 the European Green Deal, an ambitious approach to environmental protection, encompassing climate action, biodiversity conservation, and sustainable development. In 2021, as the world's third-biggest emitter, the EU pledged to cut its net emissions by 55% by 2030, from 1990 levels, which was one of the most ambitious goals among major polluters. Moreover, the EU declared climate neutrality by 2050, a goal that the climate law enshrined. The 8th Environmental Programme, covering the period from 2022 to 2030 (European Parliament, Council of the European Union, 2022), reflected to the greatest extent the EU's emphasis on climate reforms and the implementation of the Green Deal goals. It focused just on six main priorities, including adaptation to climate change, achieving a regenerative growth model, reducing pollution to zero, protecting and restoring biodiversity, and introducing sustainable production and consumption. The conditions for achieving these goals included neutral and obvious areas like digitalization, as well as the imperative of implementing the latest science and knowledge. On the other hand, the program also included politically unpopular proposals such as decreasing the Union's material and consumption footprints or phasing out fossil subsidies. It also mentioned an interest in challenging the idea of moving "beyond GDP" and using well-being as a compass for policy.

The European Environment Agency (2023), which is monitoring the implementation of the 8th EAP, indicates that only 5 out of 28 objectives have a high likelihood of implementation by 2030. These objectives include a 55% reduction in premature deaths from air pollution (compared to 2005 levels); an increase in spending by households, corporations, and governments on environmental protection; an increase in eco-innovation, green employment, and the share of the green economy in the overall economy. Others are not likely to happen, like increasing net GHG removals by carbon sinks from the land use, land use change and forestry (LULUCF) sector, lowering primary and final energy consumption by 2030, doubling the amount of materials that are reused or recycled by 2030 compared to 2020, farming 25% more land organically by 2030, and lowering the EU's consumption footprint, or the damage that consumption does to the environment. The majority of the categories are highly improbable, but their likelihood remains uncertain. The overall picture of what half of the century-long EU affords in environmental protection seems promising, although not enthusiastic. EU efforts have reduced the use of over 200 stratospheric ozone-depleting substances, reduced other air emissions, and improved urban air quality in terms of air and water pollution control. Still, particulate matter and ground-level ozone concentrations remained above EU limits, and some member states exceeded national targets. The EU water governance focuses on integrated watershed management, enhancing water quality through pollution controls with positive results. The 2019 EU Commission evaluation (European Commission, 2019) reveals that the EU collects and treats almost all wastewater to high standards, with nearly 100% collection and over 90% treatment compliance. The introduction of the circular economy presented many challenges. Each European produced approximately 4.8 tonnes of waste annually, of which about 39% underwent treatment. The EU has improved its recycling rates, recycling nearly half of its municipal waste. However, around a quarter of municipal waste still ends up in landfills. Despite an increase in waste generation by 1%, the share of waste sent to landfills decreased from 23% *to* 16% in the EU-27 between 2010 and 2020. By 2030, all EU member states will be required to recycle at least 60% of their municipal waste. In the case of GHG emissions, the EU has shown progress towards a carbon-free economy. Till 2020, economic growth was on the rise, while emissions dropped by 30% compared to 1990 levels. The energy industries were leading the way with a decrease of 47%. The only two sectors that witnessed increases were international aviation and transport (European Council, 2024).

The international environmental impact of the EU has also grown. In 2024, the EU participated in 37 environmental multilateral agreements, largely shaping them with its arguments and proposals. It also succeeded in establishing itself as a significant participant, particularly in the annual climate negotiations. Cooperation with partners within the European Neighbourhood Policy, especially candidate countries (Albania, Bosnia and Herzegovina, Georgia, Moldova, Montenegro, North Macedonia, Serbia, and Turkey), has received special importance. Nearly all 35 chapters of the acquis incorporate sustainability elements. Simultaneously, collaboration with other partners like China, India, Brazil, and other growing economies from narrowly understood trade relations, although subjected to the duty of environmental assessment (from 1999), has been sensitised to include sustainable elements like green technologies and the sharing of best practices.

Despite undeniable achievements, there exist areas that may be considered as notable failures, as written by Selin and Vandeveer (2015, p. 326). The EU's Common Agriculture Policy has been facing criticism for its high costs, subsidies to large producers, and insufficient integration of eco-concerns. Similarly, the Common Fisheries Policy has been overwhelmed by political disagreements and the neglect of scientific expertise. For example, overfishing and degradation of marine ecosystems have been hindering the EU's progress towards its biodiversity and ecosystem restoration targets. Moreover, non-compliance with EU environmental policy has created a gap between EU legislation and national policies. Parallelly, the EU had to confront multi-faced crises encompassing migration, pandemics, and energy shocks after Russian aggression in Ukraine. Besides the first one, two others can actually create opportunities for environmental protection, as they should aim at sustainable shifts in all aspects of the economy, with particular emphasis on renewable energy. Already in 2021, with the introduction of the EU's Recovery and Resilience Facility, as part of the NextGenerationEU initiative, green and digital transitions were enumerated as an opportunity to accelerate the EU's transformation.

Looking ahead, the EU's environmental policy is likely to be shaped by several key trends, including the growing urgency of climate change, technological innovation, and evolving geopolitical dynamics, mainly the situation in Eastern Europe but also tensions in the Middle East. The EU's role as a global leader in environmental protection will depend on its ability to navigate these challenges collectively and effectively, which may, however, cause internal strains.

1.3 Main actors, policy-making, instruments, and interests

As the EU lacks one organizational centre for environmental policymaking and implementation, it is also divided and cross-cuts many institutions. Five EU bodies are most actively involved: the European Council, the European Commission, the Council of the EU, the Parliament, and the Court. Every institution plays a different part in this complex and time-consuming process. The European Council, gathering the heads of state, occupies an important role in formulating collective targets for GHG emission reductions or renewable energy expansions, giving much consideration to national, political, and economic conditions, for example, the role of coal regions. The general, supranational interests are mainly represented by the Commission, which over decades has gained the status of a crucial player in crafting legislative regulations, managing EU policy and allocation of financial resources, executing laws, as well as representing EU interests outside. Each of the 27 members of the Commission – commissioners – holds responsibility for a different portfolio and is supported by an issue-specific department: Directorate-General (DG). Due to the multifaceted sources and impacts of environmental pollution, two main bodies in the area are the Directorates-General for Environment (ENV) and for Climate Action (CLIMA). They cooperate with other directorates responsible for Energy (ENER), Agriculture and Rural Development (AGRI), Economic and Financial Affairs (ECFIN), Health and Food

Safety (SANTE), Health Emergency Preparedness and Response Authority (HERA), Internal Market, Industry, Entrepreneurship, and SMEs (GROV), Maritime Affairs and Fisheries (MARE), Mobility and Transport (MOVE), and Regional and Urban Policy (REGIO). The Council is the second crucial body, but with the domination of national interests as each member state has its representative, mostly the minister responsible for specific areas. Its role is essential in coordinating member states' policies, negotiating and adopting the laws, developing common foreign and security policies, adopting the budget, and concluding international agreements. The Council holds a pivotal position in EU environmental legislation, being one of the two bodies responsible for reviewing legislative proposals from the Commission through the ordinary legislative procedure. The institution representing citizens' interests is the European Parliament, which approves EU legislation. It not only passed most of the Green Deal regulations, like the Climate Law from 2021 but also criticised the member states for their unsatisfactory level of implementation of environmental law. Finally, the European Court significantly shapes EU environmental governance by interpreting EU law, resolving conflicts, and providing guidance on its application in member states, ensuring adherence to standards across the EU. As it can settle disputes between individuals and EU bodies, it has become the arena of citizens' pleas against the norms and inertia of the EU bodies in the area of air pollution or climate protection.

This institutional architecture is constantly faced with colliding interests, not only of the member states and other EU bodies but also of private or civil society actors. Lobbying allows non-state groups to influence policy, but some worry that it gives too much power to certain interests, especially in agricultural, environmental, fisheries, and industrial policies. To balance this, environmental organizations often look for allies within the Commission, Parliament, and leading member states. All major interest groups try to influence EU policymaking through umbrella organizations, and some (Greenpeace, Friends of the Earth, WWF) have their offices in Brussels.

Environmental governance in the EU follows certain general rules that evolved over decades. As indicated by Hocaoglu (2020, p. 72), some principles are enshrined in treaties, while others are outlined in EAPs. The environmental goals set in the Treaty of Lisbon (European Union, 2007) include preserving, protecting, and enhancing environmental quality; safeguarding human health; responsible utilization of natural resources; and promoting international measures to address regional or global environmental issues. These goals grow over time to align with new developments and EU needs, like including climate change in the 6th EAP. Key principles guiding environmental policy include the polluter pays principle, subsidiarity, integration, precautionary measures, rectification at source, sustainable development, and ensuring a high level of environmental protection. These principles collectively aim to empower member states in decision-making while integrating environmental concerns across policy areas.

The EU environmental principles mostly reflect the modern type of environmental governance and are copied in many parts of the world, which also characterises the EU's set of applied environmental instruments. These can be divided into five main categories, as proposed by Böcher and Töller (2007, pp. 299–304): regulative, marked-based, procedural, cooperative, and persuasive. According to Schmitt and Schulze (2011, pp. 1–27), the character of the chosen instruments evolved over decades from traditional command and control regulation in the area of air pollution control to new, less interventionist forms of governance in the environmental dimension of EU energy policy. From 1970 to 2011, regulative instruments in air protection constituted more than half of all applied instruments and included mostly technical requirements followed by limit values and, to a lesser extent, implementation requirements, restrictions (on production or trade), allocation of emission allowances, national allocation plans, approval of procedures, and mandatory targets. The second category of most common instruments (more than 25%) included procedural ones like audits, authorization procedures, evaluation, institutional policy, monitoring, reporting, and specification of inventory systems. However, in managing the energy sector, both conventional and renewable, the most common instruments were cooperative ones, including action plans, an adaptation of legislation, commitment, financial support (demonstration projects), financial support (research), harmonization, information exchange, planning, recommendation, reporting, research, and development. Only to a minor extent, market-based (auctioning of allowances, investment prescriptions, premiums, taxes, trading schemes) and persuasive instruments (access to information, education, and training) were used. It proves that environmental policies, especially air protection policies, are still subject to traditional governance solutions, with the supplementary role of the new environmental policy instruments (NEPSs).

The political decision-making process and the selection of instruments described above are supported by the technocratic pillar, mostly by the European Environment Agency. Established in 1990 and headquartered in Copenhagen, Denmark, the EEA aims to help policymakers and the public make informed decisions about the environment. As indicated by Dammann and Gee (2011, p. 238), it is a profound example of the need for close interconnection between science and policy-making. It collects data from member countries, conducts assessments, and produces reports on various environmental topics, including air and water quality, climate change, biodiversity, and sustainable development. Additionally, the EEA facilitates collaboration between EU member states and coordinates environmental monitoring and reporting efforts. The agency gathers 32 member countries, including the 27 EU member states, Iceland, Liechtenstein, Norway, Switzerland, and Turkey. The EEA has proven to have an inclusive character as it invited all pre-2004 candidate countries to become full members. The six West Balkan countries (Albania, Bosnia and Herzegovina, North Macedonia, Montenegro, Serbia, and Kosovo) have the status of cooperating countries. There are also regional partnerships within the European Neighbourhood Policy, including countries of the Eastern Partnership, Union for the Mediterranean, and Central Asian States. Surprisingly, Great Britain, after Brexit, decided to leave most of the structures of the Agency.

Over the years, the EEA has achieved significant achievements in advancing environmental knowledge, public awareness, and first of all policy development in Europe (Turnheim et al., 2020, p. 116). The EEA reports, assessments, and data have contributed to the formulation of environmental policies and legislation at the EU level, leading to many improvements. The EEA also facilitates European nations' cooperation and knowledge exchange. The agency has contributed to the strengthening of environmental monitoring and reporting systems. Furthermore, it has made international collaboration and standardization of environmental laws and regulations easier. Simultanously, it also remained it's independent and critical position towards national and the EU policies. The Executive Director of the EEA, Leena Ylä-Mononen, admitted in 2023, following the release of the European Climate Risk Assessment that politicians at the national and European levels must take immediate action to lower climate risks by fast emission reductions as well as robust adaption plans and activities to guarantee the resilience of society (European Environment Agency, 2024b).

The European Environment Information and Observation Network (Eionet, 2024), established in 1994, serves as the partner network of the EEA. Recognized for providing high-quality data, information, and sustainability assessments throughout Europe, Eionet comprises National Focal Points, mainly national environmental agencies. These points are nominated and funded by their respective countries, enabling the network to fulfil its multifaceted role effectively. The Eionet encompasses 12 groups, mostly thematic, and 7 topic centres.

The European Union operates also several environmental information systems. They include the Marine Water Information System, the Biodiversity Information System, the European Climate and Health Observatory, Climate Adapt, the European Industrial Emissions Portal, Climate and Energy, and the Copernicus program. The last one is a comprehensive Earth Observation Programme, part of the European Union's Space program, dedicated to monitoring various aspects of the Earth's environment. It covers five main areas: air quality and atmospheric composition, ozone layer and ultraviolet radiation, emissions and surface fluxes, solar radiation, and fire radiative power and climate forcing (Copernicus, 2024).

In terms of air quality and atmospheric composition, Copernicus provides data on regulated pollutants such as nitrogen dioxide, ozone, coarse particulate matter, fine particulate matter ($PM_{2.5}$), and sulphur dioxide. It also monitors other air quality pollutants like ammonia, carbon monoxide, formaldehyde, and various volatile organic compounds (VOCs), along with allergen pollens (alder, birch, grass, mugwort, olive, ragweed), and aerosol tracers.

This program delivers country-specific, EU-wide, and sectoral data. For example, it delivers valuable data on the contributions of different countries or cities to $PM_{2.5}$ and PM_{10} levels, facilitating the assessment of air quality on both regional and local scales. It annually contributes validated reports, analyses, and projections up to 2050, which should constitute a cornerstone for long-term air quality and climate mitigation strategies. Furthermore, Copernicus offers detailed explanations for specific episodes such as ozone pollution, Saharan dust events, forest fires, high PM_{10} episodes, and the impact of events like the COVID-19 lockdown on air quality. What is even more crucial is that Copernicus data and information are available on a full, free, and open basis, enabling citizens to gain knowledge and engage in environmental actions and decision-making processes. It is also a valuable source for researchers conducting various comparative or case studies as exemplified by Pisoni et al. (2022, pp. 1–9) and their input on the EU cities' pollution.

Additionally, the European Pollutant Release and Transfer Register (E-PRTR) delivers environmental information on pollutants released into the air, water, and land. The register annually updates data from approximately 35,000 out of 50,000 facilities, covering 65 economic activities. It includes information on 91 key pollutants, such as heavy metals, pesticides, greenhouse gases, and dioxins, from EU member states, Iceland, Liechtenstein, Norway, Switzerland, Serbia, and the United Kingdom. The E-PRTR is closely linked to the Industrial Emissions Directive, with reporting requirements for pollutant releases and transfers aligned with the permit conditions. In 2019, the E-PRTR reporting requirements were updated by the Commission Implementing Decision, and amongst other changes, they obliged the member states to report by the end of November each year. In 2022, the Commission proposed to revise the E-PRTR Regulation to create the Industrial Emissions Portal, aiming to improve data transparency and public access to environmental information but it is still stuck in the negotiating process (European Commission, 2024a).

To sum up, the EU's environmental management structure is based on a constant flow of political, economic, and social stimuli. Some are horizontal, for example, bilateral or multilateral relations between member states or between different EU institutions. Others follow a vertical dimension, which can be either top-down or bottom-up. Most countries send signals/demands to EU bodies as parts of a higher governing structure, similar to interest groups attempting to impact both national and European policies. Furthermore, data flows mainly from local and national stakeholders to competent authorities, which pass it on to the EEA and the Commission before it is provided to political entities like the European Parliament or the Council. On the other hand, EU norms and regulations, formulated via a supranational process supplemented with political support but not necessarily unanimity, are applied to member states. One of the most vital and complex environmental projects of the last decade, the Green Deal, is to be discussed in the next subchapter.

1.4 Green Deal – a new vision for the 21st century?

The European Green Deal (EDG) is a strategic, long-term program established by the European Commission in December 2019. Its major goal is to make the EU economy greener, less dependent on resources, more competitive, and adaptive to the climate change problem. It is a strategy that is as complex as the social and economic problem it addresses, and which may be understood as a form of ecological modernization, an equality project, a bid for the EU to retain its leadership in the global climate change and sustainability agenda, and to strengthen its competitiveness. In other words, the EGD is a plan to change the EU to a strong economy that is sustainable, resource-efficient, and carbon-neutral by 2050. It provides stricter norms in terms of environmental protection, but first of all, it encourages the use of renewable energy sources, cleaner technology, and resource-efficient methods; it stimulates creativity and supports companies and customers to engage in sustainable projects (Pelsa & Signe, 2022, pp. 41–51).

Besides, the EGD is rooted in an equality project that was aimed at the achievement of a just transition to a green economy. Understanding that the shift to a low-carbon economy affects different social groups and geographical areas in various ways, the EGD provided measures to address the needs of social and economic adaptation of vulnerable groups, workers in sectors that will be most affected by the transition, and regions that are most dependent on the use of fossil resources. The commitment to sustainability is underlined by the creation of the Just Transition Fund, which offers specific financial assistance to the regions in question, enables the diversification of the economy, and supports the generation of new employment opportunities. In addition, the EGD sought to promote social inclusion for those mostly vulnerable, through the provision of basic needs such as access to clean and affordable energy, eradication of transport poverty, improvement of the physical environment, and support for gender equality.

Furthermore, the EGD is a planned and visionary action of the EU to maintain its global leadership in the fight against climate change and other environmental problems and a long-term goal of the EU to become a normative power. When adopting the EU 2030 climate and energy framework, the EU sought to establish itself as a global leader by setting high-level goals for carbon neutrality, renewable energy, and biodiversity, areas where the rest of the world was lagging. The EGD's focus on international cooperation and partnership pointed to the EU's desire to engage in dialogue with the rest of the world while using its diplomatic and economic muscle. It should be noted that the normative leadership was not the only motivation as the EU needed to become more competitive as its GDP gap with the USA and China was widening. According to Politica Exterior (2023), the European economy in 2008 became 10% larger than the US economy. However, by 2022, it had reduced to 23% smaller than the size it was before the pandemic. This increase in the GDP of the European Union (including the UK before Brexit) was to the tune of 21%

when calculated in dollars. The US, for instance, experienced an increase of 72%, while China's GDP grew by an astonishing 290%. Lower growth rates in Europe seem to be associated with problems in the major sectors. In the area of energy, Europe has been dependent on the imports of cheap gas from the Russian Federation and some African countries, which has placed Moscow in a position of power over the EU. This dependence not only offered Russia strong leverage against the EU but also contributed to economic crises. In the field of defence, Europe still largely relies on NATO, or in essence the US, to protect it from external aggression. The war in Ukraine in 2022 has again spurred European countries to ramp up their defence expenditure but has also forced the EU to shift towards a new paradigm regarding energy sources and energy profiles. In the field of technology, Europe does not boast large technology companies based in Europe. On the other hand, American and Chinese companies are dominating in almost all aspects of the industry right from manufacturing electronics such as chips to app development, e-commerce, and AI.

Undoubtedly, the EU required a new strategy to adopt openness and to develop a fast pace of growth for the new challenges and opportunities of the 21st century. This meant reconsidering its policies in several areas including technology and energy, defence, and security to guarantee competitiveness, innovation, and development. Indeed, the Green Deal is a comprehensive set of measures and policies in different areas to address these objectives. The central part of the strategy is the "Fit for 55" package of measures initiated in June 2021 by the European Commission and then the REPowerEU package adopted in May 2022 as the EU's reaction to the energy challenges posed by the Russian aggression against Ukraine. "Fit for 55" refers to reducing net GHG emissions by at least 55% by 2030 (including international aviation and land use, land use change, and forestry, or LULUCF). These moderate ambitions were upheld in the Nationally Determined Contributions (NDCs) submitted to the UNFCCC in October 2023. Compared to the prior NDCs from December 2020, they only raised the land sector target by 85 $MtCO_2e$ (Spain and the European Commission, 2023). However, according to Climate Action Tracker (2024), policies implemented by the individual member states would result in emissions reductions of less than 36% below 1990 levels by 2030, which is far from satisfactory and indicates a gap between national and EU-level policies. On February 6, 2024, the European Commission (2024b) proposed a 2040 target aiming for a 90% net GHG emissions reduction below 1990 levels, but it falls short of the more ambitious 90 – 95% goal recommended by the European Scientific Advisory Board on Climate Change (2023). It also lacks clarity on fossil fuel phase-out dates and carbon removal transparency.

As summed up in the NDCs updated in 2023 (Spain and the European Commission, 2023) the EU Emissions Trading System remains the main market-based mechanism designed to reduce GHG emissions by placing a cap on the total amount that can be emitted and allowing companies to buy and sell emission allowances. It was, however, revised in early 2023, increasing the targets for emissions reduction from 43% *to* 62% for the 2005–2030 period. This helps to accelerate cuts but free allowances for about 45% of industrial emissions are still available, amounting to over 4. 9 billion allowances by 2030. The EU also agreed to apply prices to carbon-intensive goods imported from third countries in the form of the Carbon Border Adjustment Mechanism. This mechanism, which will be fully functional from 2026, keeps all the revenues within the EU, which creates friction with the Global South trading partners who claim that such funds should be used to finance their transition to net-zero. Also, legislation proposed a second generation of the ETS (ETS II) for road transport and buildings to start in 2027 or 2028 depending on the price of fossil gas. It is expected to account for a 42% reduction in emissions by 2030 from the base year of 2005 in the targeted sectors and it will not provide free allowances.

The sectors that were not included in ETS such as transport, buildings, agriculture, and waste were regulated by the Effort Sharing Regulation (ESR) which was revised on 19th of April, 2023, as part of the "FitFor55" package (European Parliament, Council of the European Union 2023a). The ESR allocates emission reduction responsibilities to member states according to their GDP, with the more affluent countries having more stringent standards. For non-ETS sectors, each member state has an individual emissions reduction target in order to meet the overall emissions reduction targets of the EU. The new regulations raised the emissions reductions from 30% below 2005 levels to 40% by 2030. Targets vary from 10% for Bulgaria to 50% for several countries, with options such as borrowing and banking of emissions between years and countries. There are also new requirements for standards of emission in transport. New cars and vans from 2030 should emit 50% less CO_2 emissions, compared to 2021, and starting from 2035, they must be only emissions-free (Council of the European Union, 2023). The EU has also signed agreements on sustainable transport fuels for maritime and aviation industries and regulations to advance the deployment of alternative fuel infrastructure to decrease GHG.

In energy efficiency and renewable energy targets, the EU has set itself high standards. As for the Renewable Energy Directive, goals were first set at 32% for 2030 and then raised to 42.5% with an additional 2.5% as an indicative top-up (European Parliament, Council of the European Union, 2023b). In line with the European Commission's "RepowerEU" strategy to diversify away from Russian fossil fuels before 2030, the EU aims for an 11.7% reduction in final energy consumption by 2030. The primary energy consumption should be 993 Mtoe and the final energy consumption should be 763 Mtoe by 2030. The only binding target for final energy consumption is at the EU level, with member states obliged to fulfil an average annual decrease of 1.5% between 2024 and 2030. Member states submitted drafts of their National Energy and Climate Plans (NECPs) in 2023, but there are doubts about their level of ambition and compliance with EU goals.

The European Green Deal has also provided measures that are meant to ensure that pollution levels are brought to zero in different sectors. The Chemical Strategy for Sustainability is one of the key programs aimed at improving the protection of people and the environment from dangerous chemicals. Also, the Zero Pollution Action Plan focuses on enhancing the quality of water, air, and soil through prevention, clean-up, control, assessment, and reporting of pollution (European Commission, 2021). Steps are also being taken to review the measures to control pollution from large industrial installations in the light of new climate, energy, and circular economy policies. The Action Plan assumes to step up pollution prevention at the source till 2030. The specific targets include reducing the number of premature deaths due to air pollution by 55%, increasing the quality of water, decreasing waste and sea-based plastic litter by 50%, and reducing the environmental microplastic emissions by 30%. It also seeks to enhance the quality of the soil by cutting nutrient losses and chemical pesticide usage by 50% . Finally, the plan aims at a substantial reduction in waste production and a 50% reduction in residual municipal waste.

As part of the European Green Deal, the European Commission introduced the "Farm to Fork" Strategy in May 2020 (European Commission, 2020). This strategy aims to improve the sustainability of the food supply chains by better control over every phase, from production to consumption, with a strong emphasis on reducing food loss and waste. It is complemented by other key initiatives such as the Methane Strategy, the Circular Economy Action Plan, the Biodiversity Strategy, and the Adaptation Strategy. It seeks to reduce the overall use and risks of chemical pesticides by 50% by 2030 and phase out high-risk pesticides entirely by the same year. The strategy also aims to allocate at least 10% of agricultural land to highly diverse landscape features, ensure that 25% of the EU's agricultural land is organic by 2030, cut nutrient losses by at least 50% without compromising soil fertility, and reduce fertilizer use by at least 20% by 2030 (European Commission, 2020). These objectives respond to both internal and external pressures. European citizens, increasingly concerned about health issues linked to diet, and suffering from obesity (more than 50% of the population) have a stronger awareness of the food quality. The COVID-19 pandemic further spotlighted existing challenges, such as disruptions in international food chains and the role of third countries in the global food system. The overarching aim is to elevate European food to a global standard of quality, health, and organic production, providing European farmers – a significant and influential group – with a competitive advantage and opening up new business opportunities. However, the EU has yet to reach a consensus on a Sustainable Food Systems Law that would comprehensively address these challenges. The decision has been postponed until after the European Parliament elections in June 2024 (European Commission, 2024c).

All the above-discussed actions and decisions undoubtedly prove that the EGD is a significant turning point towards sustainability and climate change in the EU. Although the concept of the EGD is quite noble, its execution is not without its difficulties, which must be overcome for the plan to work. One of the major issues is that the strategy is long-term, and critics have pointed out that it does not pay enough attention to short-term measures. This approach can lead to the impression of doing nothing, especially when immediate action is required to address the worsening climate crisis. However, the major challenge is that the member states have different interests. The process of forming coalitions with countries that have different goals and levels of development is always a difficult task, which needs diplomatic skills and negotiations. There are also financial concerns that need to be taken into consideration. Issues regarding cost accountability remain ambiguous, and there are questions about how the project will stay on schedule. The notion of the first-mover advantage is becoming less relevant as other continents follow or even overtake the EU's actions. Unfortunately, the marginal role of cities, which are typically the most active agents in implementing sustainable innovations, is obvious. They still lack sufficient administrative and political representation within the decision-making processes. Moreover, the fact that the EGD is built on the concept of growth is questionable. Growth is crucial for economic stability, but it is not necessarily aligned with sustainability objectives, particularly when it goes beyond the planetary boundaries discussed earlier.

Looking at the main projects of the EGD, it is clear that the agreement only covers 12 of the 17 SDGs listed in the 2030 Sustainable Development Agenda (SDA). Even these elaborated areas are not fully put into action. Alarms over the EU's Paris Agreement targets have been raised by independent evaluations like the Climate Action Tracker (2024). Particularly concerning the target of keeping warming well below 2°C, the EU's efforts are seen to be insufficient in achieving fair emissions distribution. This emphasises how much more help – financial assistance included – is required for developing countries to cut emissions. Furthermore, the social effects of the EGD on the trading partners of the EU are still mostly ignored. Non-EU producers, farmers, and labourers have not received clear acknowledgment of the support, making the danger of making power imbalances already present worse, especially in weak global supply chains (Ponthieu, Vernier, Lunder, & Conesa, 2023, pp. 1–10).

The future of the EGD is closely related to several variables. Individual national positions within the EU spectrum – from enthusiastic proponents to hesitant laggards – will be very important. The course of the EGD may also be shaped by unanticipated "Black Swans", technological breakthroughs, and international developments. Maybe, most importantly, the 2024 European Parliament elections and the creation of a new Commission will condition further developments. The choices taken politically at these critical junctures will either increase the momentum of the EGD or present new difficulties. Despite the new political landscape, the EGDs will need to be navigated and supported by both the determined institutions and the ambitions and potentials of individual member states.

Reference list

Atomic Heritage Foundation. (2024). *The Russell-Einstein manifesto*. Retrieved July 9, 1955, from https://ahf.nuclearmuseum.org/ahf/key-documents/russell-einstein-manifesto/

Benson, D., & Jordan, A. (2010). European Union environmental policy after the Lisbon. *Environmental Politics, 19*(3), 468–474.

Böcher, M., & Töller, A. (2007). Instrumentenwahl und Instrumentenwandel in der Umweltpolitik. Ein theoretischer Erklärungsrahmen. In K. Jacob, F. Biermann, P. Busch & P. Feindt (Eds.), *PVS-Sonderheft. Politik und Umwelt, 39* (pp. 299–322). Vs Verlag Für Sozialwissenschaften.

Burchell, J., & Lightfoot, S. (2001). *The greening of the European Union?* Sheffield Academic Press.

Climate Action Tracker. (2024). *European Union. Country summary*. https://climateactiontracker.org/countries/eu/targets/

Copernicus. (2024). https://atmosphere.copernicus.eu/

Council of the European Union. (2023). *'Fit for 55': Council adopts regulation on CO$_2$ emissions for new cars and vans*. Press release. Retrieved March 28, 2023, from https://www.consilium.europa.eu/en/press/press-releases/2023/03/28/fit-for-55-council-adopts-regulation-on-co2-emissions-for-new-cars-and-vans/

Dammann, S., & Gee, D. (2011). Science into policy: The European Environment Agency. In J. Lentsch & P. Weingart (Eds.), *The politics of scientific advice. Institutional design for quality assurance* (pp. 238–258). Cambridge University Press.

Eionet. (2024). https://www.eionet.europa.eu/

Elhacham, E., Ben-Uri, L., Grozovski, J., Bar-On, Y. M., & Milo, R. (2020). Global human-made mass exceeds all living biomass. *Nature, 588*(7838), 442–444.

European Commission. (2019, May 15). *Report from the commission to the European Parliament, the Council, the European Economic and Social Committee, and the Committee of the Regions on the Evaluation of the 7th Environment Action Programme {SWD(2019) 181 final}*. Brussels, COM(2019) 233 final. https://data.consilium.europa.eu/doc/document/ST-9416-2019-INIT/en/pdf

European Commission. (2020). *Communication from the commission to the European Parliament, the Council, the European Economic and Social Committee, and the Committee of the Regions. A farm to fork strategy for a fair, healthy, and environmentally-friendly food system*. COM/2020/381 final. https://eur-lex.europa.eu/legal-content/EN/TXT/?uri=CELEX:52020DC0381

European Commission. (2021). *Communication from the commission to the European Parliament, the Council, the European Economic and Social Committee, and the Committee of the Regions Pathway to a Healthy Planet for All. EU action plan: 'Towards zero pollution for air, water and soil'*. Com/2021/400 Final. https://eur-lex.europa.eu/legal-content/EN/ALL/?uri=COM%3A2021%3A400%3AFIN

European Commission. (2022). *Zero pollution: New rules for healthy air*. Fact sheet. https://ec.europa.eu/commission/presscorner/api/files/attachment/873813/Factsheet%20on%20Air%20Quality_EN.pdf.pdf

26 *Katarzyna Dośpiał-Borysiak*

European Commission. (2024a). *The European pollutant release and transfer register (E-PRTR)*. https://environment.ec.europa.eu/topics/industrial-emissions-and-safety/european-pollutant-release-and-transfer-register-e-prtr_en

European Commission. (2024b). *Communication from the commission to the European Parliament, the Council, the European Economic and Social Committee and the Committee of the Regions. Securing our future. Europe's 2040 climate target and path to climate neutrality by 2050 building a sustainable, just and prosperous society.* COM(2024) 63 final. https://eur-lex.europa.eu/legal-content/EN/TXT/?uri=COM%3A2024%3A63%3AFIN

European Commission. (2024c). *The legislative framework for sustainable food systems.* https://food.ec.europa.eu/horizontal-topics/farm-fork-strategy/legislative-framework_en

European Council. (2024). *Policies.* https://www.consilium.europa.eu/en/policies/

European Environment Agency. (2023). *European Union 8th environment action programme monitoring report on progress towards the 8th EAP objectives 2023 edition.* Report 11. https://www.eea.europa.eu/publications/european-union-8th-environment-action-programme

European Environment Agency. (2024). *Europe is not prepared for rapidly growing climate risks.* Press release. Retrieved March 11, 2024, from https://www.eea.europa.eu/en/newsroom/news/europe-is-not-prepared-for

European Parliament, Council of the European Union. (2013). *Decision no 1386/2013/EU of the European Parliament and of the Council of 20 November 2013 on a general union environment action programme to, 2020 living well, within the limits of our planet.* https://eur-lex.europa.eu/legal-content/EN/TXT/?uri=CELEX:32013D1386

European Parliament, Council of the European Union. (2022). *Decision (EU) 2022/591 of the European Parliament and of the Council of 6 April 2022 on a general union environment action programme to 2030.* https://eur-lex.europa.eu/legal-content/EN/TXT/?uri=CELEX:32022D0591

European Parliament, Council of the European Union. (2023a). *Regulation (EU) 2023/857 of the European Parliament and of the Council of 19 April 2023 amending Regulation (EU) 2018/842 on binding annual greenhouse gas emission reductions by Member States from 2021 to 2030 contributing to climate action to meet commitments under the Paris Agreement, and Regulation (EU) 2018/1999 (Text with EEA relevance).* Official Journal of the European Union, L 111/1.

European Parliament, Council of the European Union. (2023b). *Regulation (EU) 2023/857 of the European Parliament and of the Council of 19 April 2023 amending regulation (EU) 2018/842 on binding annual greenhouse gas emission reductions by member states from 2021 to 2030 contributing to climate action to meet commitments under the Paris agreement, and regulation (EU) 2018/1999 (Text with EEA relevance).* PE/72/2022/REV/1. Official Journal of the European Union, L 111/1.

European Scientific Advisory Board on Climate Change. (2023). Scientific advice for the determination of an EU-wide 2040 climate target and a greenhouse gas budget for 2030–2050. Luxembourg: Publications Office of the European Union. https://doi.org//10.2800/609405.

European Union. (2007). *Treaty of Lisbon amending the treaty on European Union and the treaty establishing the European Community, signed at Lisbon, 13 December 2007*. Official Journal of the European Union, C 306/1.

Hector, D., Christensen, C., & Petrie, J. (2014). Sustainability and sustainable development: Philosophical distinctions and practical implications. *Environmental Values*, *23*(1), 7–28.

Hocaoglu, B. (2020). The environmental policy decision making process in the EU. *Ekonomik Toplumsal Siyasal Analiz*, *5*, 71–86. https://www.researchgate.net/publication/343787671_The_Environmental_Policy_Decision_Making_Process_in_the_EU

Inglehart, R. (1977). *The silent revolution: Changing values and political styles among western publics*. Princeton University Press.

Meadows, D. H, Meadows, D. L., Randers, J., & Behrens, W. (1972). *Limits to the growth. Report for the club of Rome project on the predicament of mankind*. Universe Books.

Millennium Development Goals Monitor. (2015). https://www.mdgmonitor.org/millennium-development-goals/page/2/

Ossewaarde, M., & Ossewaarde-Lowtoo, R. (2020). The EU's Green Deal: A third alternative to green growth and degrowth. *Sustainability*, *12*(23), 9825. https://www.mdpi.com/2071-1050/12/23/9825

Pelsa, I., & Signe, B. (2022). Main priorities for a Green Deal towards a climate-neutral. *European Integration Studies*, *1*, 41–51.

Pisoni, E., Thunis, P., De Meij., A., Bessagnet., B., & Pommier., M. (2022). Use of the Copernicus atmosphere monitoring service policy products to evaluate the contribution of EU cities to their pollution. *Atmospheric Environment*, *X*, *16*, 100194. https://doi.org/10.1016/j.aeaoa.2022.100194

Politica Exterior. (2023, July 26). *¿Una Europa vasalla de EEUU?* https://www.politicaexterior.com/articulo/una-europa-vasalla-de-eeuu/

Ponthieu, E., Vernier Ch., Lunder., E., & Conesa., J. (2023). Fair trade principles can transform the European Green Deal: Moving towards a global Green Deal. *Journal of Fair Trade*, *4*(2), 1–10. https://doi.org/10.13169/jfairtrade.4.2.0001

Richardson, K., Steffen, W., Lucht, W., Bendtsen, J., Cornell, S. E., Donges, J. F., Drüke, M., Fetzer, I., Bala, G., von Bloh, W., Feulner, G., Fiedler, S., Gerten, D., Gleeson, T., Hofmann, M., Huiskamp, W., Kummu, M., Mohan, C., Nogués-Bravo, D., Petri, S., . . Rockström, J. (2023). Earth beyond six of nine planetary boundaries. *Science Advances*, *9*(37), eadh2458. https://doi.org/10.1126/sciadv.adh2458

Ritchie, H., Rosado, P., & Roser, M. (2024). Energy production and consumption. *Our World in Data*. https://ourworldindata.org/energy-production-consumption

Schmitt, S., & Schulze, K. (2011). Choosing environmental policy instruments: An assessment of the 'environmental dimension' of EU energy policy. In J. Tosun & I. Solorio (Eds.), *Energy and environment in Europe: Assessing a complex relationship?* European Integration Online Papers (EIoP). Special Mini-Issue, *1*(15), 1–27. http://eiop.or.at/eiop/texte/2011-009a.htm

Schumacher, E. (1973). *Small is beautiful: A study of economics as if people mattered*. Blond & Briggs.

Selin, H., & Vandeveer, S. (2015). Broader, deeper and greener: European Union environmental politics, policies, and outcomes. *Annual Review of Environment and Resources, 40*, 309–335.

Spain and the European Commission (2023). *Update of the NDC of the European Union and its member states.* https://unfccc.int/sites/default/files/NDC/2023-10/ES-2023-10-17%20EU%20submission%20NDC%20update.pdf

Turnheim, B., Asquith, M., & Geels, F. (2020). Making sustainability transitions research policy-relevant: Challenges at the science-policy interface. *Environmental Innovation and Societal Transitions, 34*, 116–120. https://doi.org/10.1016/j.eist.2019.12.009

United Nations. (1987). *Report of the world commission on environment and development: Our common future.* https://sustainabledevelopment.un.org/content/documents/5987our-common-future.pdf

United Nations. (1992). *United Nations framework convention on climate change.* https://unfccc.int/resource/docs/convkp/conveng.pdf

United Nations. (2015). *Resolution adopted by the General Assembly on 25 September 2015. Transforming our world: A sustainable development agenda for 2030.* General Assembly. A/RES/70/1. https://documents.un.org/doc/undoc/gen/n15/291/89/pdf/n1529189.pdf?token=Rsto9YNbPidycRl1z3&fe=true

United Nations. (2023). *Ensure sustainable production and consumption.* https://www.un.org/sustainabledevelopment/wp-content/uploads/2023/08/2309739_E_SDG_2023_infographics-12-12.pdf

United Nations. (2024). *Population.* https://www.un.org/en/global-issues/population

2 Ever cleaner union and the air protection concept

Katarzyna Dośpiał-Borysiak

2.1 The evolution of global air protection regime

The history of air protection dates back to medieval times as a rather local and marginal issue, typical to large population congestions. It was industrialization and urbanization that made air pollution a widely recognized phenomenon, that needs fast political engagement. Initially, the problem primarily affected the United States (US) and Europe. Until 1970, these two continents accounted for over 80% of global sulphur dioxide (SO_2) emissions, a by-product of burning fossil fuels like coal and oil in power plants, industrial facilities, and other processes such as metal smelting and oil refining. Individual consumption needs also significantly contributed to the increase in pollutants. These were primarily emitted from vehicle exhausts, especially those powered by internal combustion engines using fossil fuels like gasoline and diesel. In the US alone, nearly 100 million vehicles filled American roads by 1970. As a consequence, the visible increase in most major pollutants emissions such as nitrogen oxides (NO_x), particulate matter (PM), carbon monoxide (CO), volatile organic compounds (VOCs), and greenhouse gases (GHGs) like carbon dioxide (CO_2) and methane (CH_4) accompanied constant economic growth.

As a result, in the 1950s and 1960s, visible impacts of pollution such as smog episodes and soot-covered buildings raised public concern, awareness, and sometimes, outcry. The 1952 Great Smog of London, one of the deadliest air pollution events in history, catalysed public interest and government action. This smog, caused by a combination of industrial emissions and domestic coal burning, resulted in thousands of deaths and widespread respiratory illnesses. Similarly, the Donora smog incident, in Pennsylvania in 1948 leading to numerous deaths and illnesses, highlighted the urgent need for air quality regulation. Other incidents occurred due to specific location conditions like basin location in the case of Los Angeles or specific weather conditions like in New York.

One of the most visible and pressing problems of the period was the acid rain. The long-range acidic pollutants, primarily SO_2 and NO_x, were released

DOI: 10.4324/9781032707006-3

into the atmosphere primarily by power plants in the US and Europe, forming sulfuric and nitric acids when they combined with water vapour. As a result, acid rain harmed ecosystems, damaged buildings, and monuments, and had adverse effects on human health. Simultaneously, in the 1980s, a concerning trend of accelerated forest loss emerged in several European countries, notably in the Czech Republic, Poland, and Germany. This attracted the scientific community's interest in deteriorating forest health and prompted investigations into the relationship between declining air quality and deforestation. Simultaneously, as an understanding of air pollution deepened, attention turned to NO_x as a particularly hazardous pollutant, surpassing even sulphur in significance. Almost 95% of NO_x emissions were generated by human activities, such as burning coal, gasoline, and oil in vehicles, homes, industries, and power plants. The Netherlands and the UK were among the first to observe anomalous changes in the botanical species composition of heathlands, indicating the detrimental impact of nitrogen deposition on ecosystems. Soon eutrophication become a visible problem in other parts of Europe, as well as Asia, mainly in China (Igini, 2022). Another challenge was the ozone hole, primarily located over Antarctica. Here, the ozone layer, which protects from the sun's harmful rays, was very thin because of certain chemicals like chlorofluorocarbons (CFCs) getting released into the air. This thinning allowed more harmful ultraviolet (UV) to reach the Earth, which was dangerous for both human beings and nature.

Science and study have also brought attention to the issue of air pollution on a global scale. For instance, important data relating air pollution to detrimental health impacts was first published by Shy et al. in 1978. Research has shown the damaging effects of pollutants such as SO_2, NO_x, and PM on cardiovascular health, respiratory health, and general well-being (Chivian et al., 1993). This scientific impact was crucial in influencing public opinion and guiding legislative responses to air quality problems. Concurrently, the 1960s and 1970s witnessed the rise of the environmental movement, which demonstrated growing political demands. Stronger environmental laws and stricter air standards were pushed for by grassroots organizations and environmental advocacy groups.

Finally, the role of media in reporting and covering environmental issues, including air pollution, is impossible to overestimate. Numerous news, documentaries, and investigations have brought the extent of the problem and pollution's impact on different communities, ecosystems, and population health to the general public attention. The increased discourse around the issue has been instrumental in changing the public attitude from ignorance or denial to the understanding that immediate efforts are required.

The industries and policymakers initially resisted the call for international cooperation to combat transboundary air pollution. However, countries and nations took up the opportunity to develop their legislation, including the British Clean Air Act of 1956, and the Clean Air Act of 1970 in the US, which stipulated that states ensure the installation of governors that could shut down vehicles not complying with the set regulations. The United States CAA1970 led to significant emission reductions and the closing down of emission-heavy facilities.

Although these national and political actions served as important milestones in fighting air pollution, it was still necessary to unite the efforts of the international community. The first major milestone in this direction was represented by the Stockholm Convention of 1972, primarily focused on persistent organic pollutants (POPs,) and the protection of human health and the environment. Although the main attention was not on air quality but on POPs, it can be considered the first significant attempt to unite international efforts towards the environmental agenda. The most important milestone in this direction was represented by the establishment of the Convention on Long-Range Transboundary Air Pollution in 1979, functioning under the United Nations Economic Commission for Europe – UNECE (UNECE, 1979). The Convention, therefore, set a framework for nations to coordinate their efforts to regulate emissions of harmful pollutants, including SO_2 and NO_x, which was instrumental in future attempts to improve regional air quality. It is noteworthy that this is one of the few examples of an international agreement that united the US and the Soviet Union.

In 1987, the world saw the introduction of the Montreal Protocol, initially designed to safeguard the ozone layer by phasing out ozone-depleting substances (ODSs). While its primary focus was on ozone protection, the protocol indirectly contributed to advancements in air quality. By reducing emissions of ODSs like chlorofluorocarbons (CFCs), the Montreal Protocol helped mitigate their adverse effects on human health and ecosystems, thereby promoting air quality enhancement as a secondary benefit.

These early initiatives marked crucial steps forward in addressing air pollution at both regional and global levels, setting the stage for further advancements in air protection regimes. On the global platform, several key agreements were established to address transboundary air pollution and promote wide cooperation. The United Nations Framework Convention on Climate Change (UNFCCC), adopted in 1992, laid the groundwork for international efforts to combat climate change, including reducing GHG emissions that contribute to air pollution and global warming. Similarly, the Kyoto Protocol, adopted in 1997, set binding targets for industrialized countries to reduce their emissions of greenhouse gases.

The 1990s undoubtedly witnessed notable challenges in air protection despite visible advancements. Accelerated industrialization and urbanization globally led to a rise in emissions of air pollutants, posing significant health hazards mostly to metropolitan regions, whose size and number have grown immensely. The growing megapolises in India, China, and other developing countries revealed the necessity of sustainable urban planning. Furthermore, the open global market caused governing difficulties, as emissions from one nation could harmfully affect air quality in neighbouring countries. This also initiated a discussion about the responsibilities and duties of polluters versus victims. While emissions of most primary pollutants declined substantially in Europe, North America, and Japan during this period, with particularly significant reductions in SO_2, emissions surged in East and South Asia and other regions from 1990 to 2010, This resulted in only modest reductions in global total emissions, including SO_2, which decreased by just 15% from its peak in 1990 (Hoesly et al., 2018, p. 406).

In the early 1990s, the connections between human mortality and air pollutants, particularly PM were massively revealed. More, both political and scientific focus have been dedicated to human health concerns, like respiratory diseases, cardiovascular issues, and even premature mortality. PM, encompassing solid and liquid particles suspended in the air, spanned a wide size range and diverse chemical composition, significantly impacting human health and contributing to the long-range transport of pollutants. European Environment Agency (2007, p. 5) found $PM_{2.5}$ to be the main threat to human health from air pollution in Europe. Moreover, it has been observed that PM altered Earth's energy equilibrium through absorption, notably by substances like black carbon, as well as through the dispersion and reflection of radiation. Consequently, the connection between air quality and climate change rose from the interplay between PMs and the radiative balance. As sulphur emissions have fallen, ammonia emitted from agricultural activity and NO_x from combustion processes has become the predominant acidifying and atrophying agents affecting ecosystems.

In the 2000s, this trend continued. The political focus persisted in prioritizing human health concerns, particularly regarding exposure to PM and NO_2 in urban areas across developed and developing nations. However, the disproportionate emission burden has been moved from the initial beneficiaries of the Industrial Revolution to countries in East and South Asia. Nevertheless, the majority of the global population resided in areas where ambient $PM_{2.5}$ levels surpassed the recommended norms. For NO_x emissions, the global total continued to rise, and reductions in emissions observed in Europe, North America, and other regions were offset by increases elsewhere, primarily in Asia. Similarly, for ammonia (NH_3) and VOC, the trend mirrored that of NO_x, with a steady global increase in total emissions.

The new millennium exposed a clear attempt of the European countries to be at the forefront of combating air pollution. The Gothenburg Protocol (UNECE, 2024a), also known as the Protocol to Abate Acidification, Eutrophication, and Ground-level Ozone, was signed in 1999 (amended in 2012, with annexes from 2013 and 2017) by numerous countries in Europe (members of the European Union EU-27, Great Britain, Norway Lichtenstein, Iceland, Switzerland, and Turkey).

The UN Economic Commission for Europe played a key role in guiding the discussions that led to the adoption of the protocol. This protocol was an offshoot of the Convention on Long-Range Transboundary Air Pollution and it established specific, legally enforceable targets for slashing the output levels of what it deemed to be pivotal air pollutants. These pollutants included sulphur dioxide, NO_x, ammonia, and VOCs – all infamous for their adverse effects on both human health and the environment at large. Countries that were part of this commitment pledged to adopt anti-emission measures in industries, transport systems, or agricultural practices. The protocol emphasized the need for cooperation and collective action in the spirit of the shared responsibility of nations. The vivid examples can be found today, like collaboration with Georgia within the EU-funded "Air Quality for Better Citizen's Health" launched in April 2024. The EU also introduced crucial air quality directives to be discussed later.

Over the years, the Convention on Long-Range Transboundary Air Pollution expanded from 32 countries to 53 with new signatories like Albania, Armenia, Croatia, Kazakhstan, Kirgizstan, Malta, and Serbia. However, the process of ratification had been long and the Protocol entered into force finally in 2019. Over the three decades, it broadened the scope of its ambition and included eight protocols on the Reduction of Sulphur Emissions or their Transboundary Fluxes by at least 30% (1987); Long-term Financing of the Cooperative Programme for Monitoring and Evaluation of the Long-range Transmission of Air Pollutants in Europe (EMEP) (1987); the Control of Nitrogen Oxides or their Transboundary Fluxes (1991), the Control of Emissions of Volatile Organic Compounds or their Transboundary Fluxes (1997), Further Reduction of Sulphur Emissions (1998); Heavy Metals (2003, amended 2022); Persistent Organic Pollutants (POPs) (2003, amended 2022); and to Abate Acidification, Eutrophication and Ground-level Ozone (2005, amended in 2019 (UNECE, 2024b). It has been also institutionalized by the establishment of a Forum for collaboration on reducing air pollution (2019), with the Task Force led by Sweden and Great Britain (2021). Independently, regional collaborations appeared like cooperation under the Canada-United States Air Quality Agreement and efforts to introduce the best available techniques in Eastern Europe, the Caucasus, and Central Asia.

The 2016 Assessment Report (UNECE, 2016) clearly showed that the Convention had delivered demonstrable improvements in reducing acidification of the environment and the highest peak levels of ozone and photochemical smog, persistent organic pollutants, and heavy metals, and had begun to reduce PM and atmospheric levels and deposition of nitrogen. Global sulphur emissions have significantly decreased since their peak in 2000; SO_2 emissions in Europe and North America decreased by around 90% from their highest levels in the 1970s and 1980s, respectively, by the year 2016. Likewise, China's NO_x emissions fell by about 25% in the second decade of the 20th century, despite rising surface ozone levels. Efforts to reduce coal and oil consumption due to climate change policies are expected to further reduce SO_2 and nitrogen dioxide emissions. However, emissions reductions may be offset by challenges arising from increased ammonia emissions leading to PM and eutrophication. Furthermore, CH4 and VOC emissions are increasing, although uncertainty remains about their impacts (Fowler et al., 2020). Addressing these challenges requires international agreements recognizing the complex interactions between emissions, climate change, and forestry and land-use practices (UNECE, 2018). While substantial progress has been made in some regions, such as Asia, other areas like Africa are facing increasing air pollution challenges as their economies develop. As parts of Asia now show substantial reductions in emissions, efforts to combat climate change and increase renewable energy usage in developing regions, particularly Africa, may significantly mitigate emissions of air pollutants. The progress made recently in the realm of air protection is firmly grounded with norms, regulations, and increased consciousness about what it entails. The World Health Organization (WHO) has been a major player in the sphere of air protection as it sets emissions standards and gives guidance on pollutants in the air. Since its initial release in 1987, the WHO regularly updated its air quality guidelines, with the most recent revision occurring in 2021 (World Health Organization, 2021). These guidelines cover a range of pollutants including PM, ozone, nitrogen dioxide, sulphur dioxide, and CO.

The Montreal Protocol proved also to be effective in curbing the depletion of the ozone layer. The protocol's robust regulatory framework, which included binding targets for ozone-depleting substances (ODSs) like chlorofluorocarbons (CFCs) and halons phase-out and mechanisms for monitoring and compliance, ensured that countries adhered to their commitments. In effect, model predictions indicate that the Antarctic ozone layer can mostly recover by 2040 (NASA Earth Observatory, 2024).

Moreover, cutting-edge innovations in technology have also contributed significantly to the global monitoring of pollution in the lower part of Earth's atmosphere. The Measurements of Pollution in the Troposphere (MOPITT) and Scanning Imaging Absorption Spectrometer for Atmospheric Cartography (SCIAMACHY) instruments have delivered more than two decades' worth of data on tropospheric CO levels through satellite remote sensing – while the detection of NH_3 emissions has been made possible by the Atmospheric Infrared Sounder (AIRS) from NASA and Infrared Atmospheric Sounding Interferometer (IASI) from EUMETSAT.

Recent studies by Fowler et al. (2020) offer a modestly optimistic outlook on global air quality trends, particularly concerning two significant air pollutants: SO_2 and NO_x. Concurrently, research conducted by Li et al. (2023) indicates a notable decrease in ambient fine PM ($PM_{2.5}$) levels from 1998 to a peak in 2011, followed by a steady decline thereafter.

As economies mature, continued efforts to control emissions, particularly from combustion sources, have led to significant reductions in emissions in parts of Asia. Furthermore, there is cautious optimism about the potential of measures to combat climate change and promote the deployment of renewable energy, particularly in developing regions, to significantly reduce air pollutant emissions as these economies continue to develop. Additionally, addressing current challenges in the nitrogen cycle, particularly ammonia emissions, has the potential to improve global air quality. While controlling VOC emissions poses challenges and uncertainties, advances in emissions control technology and changes in the low-NO$_x$ chemical climate may reduce the importance of VOC emissions over time.

Undoubtedly, the global air protection regime, discussed above, significantly impacted national and international policies and practices in addressing air quality challenges and promoting emission control measures worldwide. It has also influenced EU policies in this domain by providing benchmarks, standards, and best practices for air quality management and emission controls.

2.2 The EU legislation on air protection

One of the main goals of the European Union is to guarantee clean air and safeguard public health and the environment from the harmful impacts of air pollution. As stated in the Seventh Environment Action Programme (7th EAP) (European Parliament, Council of the European Union, 2013) of 2013, the organization aims to attain levels of air quality that do not pose risks to human health and the environment, namely meeting the air quality guideline values of the World Health Organization (WHO). Achieving this goal requires vigorous air quality policies that operate effectively at various levels: global, European, national, and local, and must be well grounded in European legislation.

At the global level, the EU has harmonized its air protection policies with internationally recognized standards and guidelines, such as those of WHO. Moreover, within the framework of the UN Environmental Programme (UNEP), the EU participates in initiatives aimed at achieving zero pollution and promoting a pollution-free planet. It is also a member of the Climate and Clean Air Coalition of more than 160 governments identifying synergies between climate and clean air agendas.

The most important international treaty in the sphere of clean air is the UNECE Convention on Long-Range Transboundary Air Pollution (UNECE, 1979), also known as the Air Convention, elaborated earlier. The EU is a signatory to seven of the eight protocols that have been appended to the convention. Notably, the Gothenburg Protocol which was signed in November 1999 and revised in 2012 has a significant function. This protocol sets out emission reduction levels for 2020 and beyond, which have been integrated into EU legislation through the Directive on National Emission Reduction Plans. The amended Gothenburg Protocol was ratified by the Council Decision in 2017 after the introduction of the Commission's Clean Air Policy Package.

The EU also plays an active role in the ratification and enforcement of these protocols by other Parties. For instance, the EU provides funding for capacity-building in the areas of Eastern Europe, Caucasus, and Central Asia to help them advance in the process of ratification and implementation of the goals of the Convention. There are other examples of EU regional action to protect air quality. For example, the EU is working with the Arctic Council through its Monitoring and Assessment Program to address specific issues such as black carbon emissions affecting the Arctic region. Furthermore, the EU's Neighbourhood Policy includes several programs, such as the Balkan Green Agenda, aimed at combating air pollution outside the EU.

The guiding principle for formulation and implementation of the EU's air quality policies is subsidiarity reflecting the wider logic of multi-level governance. This principle emphasizes that decisions should be made at the most appropriate level of government, taking into account the specific needs and circumstances of different regions and communities. The EU's political efforts are based on three main pillars. The first pillar is the Air Quality Guidelines set air quality standards for ground-level ozone, PM, NO_x, harmful heavy metals, and a variety of other pollutants. Starting in 2005 or 2010, all member states must comply uniformly with these air quality standards across their territories, depending on the pollutants involved. If specified limits are exceeded, member states must develop an air quality plan setting out appropriate measures to minimize the duration of the exceedance.

The second pillar encompasses national emission reduction objectives outlined in the National Emissions Ceiling Directive from 2016 for five key transboundary air pollutants – sulphur oxides, NO_x, non-CH_4VOC, ammonia and primary fine PM of 2.5 microns or less in diameter ($PM_{2.5}$). These national emissions reduction targets have been updated to include new thresholds to be achieved first till 2020 and then till 2030. Member states were required to develop national air pollution control plans by 2019 to ensure compliance with their emission reduction commitments. Reporting requirements and emissions reduction commitments are based on national energy consumption and fuel sales. Air quality plans are mandatory in areas with exceeded air quality standards or where there's a risk of surpassing them, namely polluted areas and agglomerations. In several member states, local governments are tasked by national authorities with the development and execution of these plans (European Parliament, Council of the European Union, 2016).

The European Union legislation grants member states the autonomy to determine the methods by which they comply with the limit values established at the EU level (European Environment Agency, 2023). However, for significant sources of pollution, standardized EU-level regulations are imposed to facilitate the smooth functioning of the internal market. Governments create and enforce laws and regulations to control emissions from industrial facilities, transportation, agriculture, and other sources. They also set up monitoring networks to assess air quality and track progress towards air quality goals. The model for air defence management depends on the member state and can be more centralized, with the main obligations falling on national governments, or decentralized, providing greater flexibility to local authorities.

Regardless of the division of tasks, ultimate responsibility for compliance with EU directives rests solely with the central government, and infringement proceedings cannot be brought against individual regions or cities.

The third pillar encompasses emissions regulations for significant sources of pollution, spanning from vehicle and ship emissions to energy and industrial sectors. These standards are established at the EU level through legislation addressing industrial emissions, power plant emissions, vehicle emissions, fuels as well as handling and storage of fuel, and the energy efficiency of products including design standards for certain equipment such as domestic stoves (European Commission, 2018).

All of the above-described pillars have emerged gradually over time due to the growing awareness of the health and environmental impact of economic development. The first attempts to regulate air protection in the EU were made due to the increasing concern about industrialization and urbanization processes, and later due to the climate change issues. The first major step towards EU emissions control was made in 1979 with Directive 79/939/EEC, which aimed at controlling emissions of SO_2 and PM from large combustion plants. Other measures in the 1980s were the implementation of the Acid Rain Directive (Directive 80/779/EEC) that dealt with the problem of air pollution and its impact in the form of acid rain. The first Clean Air Programme of the EU was set up in 1987, which aimed at a comprehensive approach to air pollution control, with a special emphasis on emission control from industries, vehicles, and the energy sector. In 1990, the National Emissions Ceilings Directive (Directive 90/90/EEC) was adopted to establish emission reduction commitments for member states, to reduce emissions of sulphur dioxide, NO_x, and other pollutants.

These early measures paved the way for more development of air protection, which showed the EU's concern for the environment and the health of the citizens. When the idea of ecological modernization began to take root, attempts were made to incorporate environmentalism into economic strategies and manufacturing processes. This approach stressed the need to introduce cleaner technologies, encourage the use of renewable energy, and integrate sustainable urban development to reduce air pollution and enhance economic development. Furthermore, increasing public awareness of the health and environmental consequences of air pollution emerged as a critical objective, which resulted in the initiation of campaigns and educational programs that would help to encourage behavioural changes and foster a culture of environmental responsibility among citizens.

The EU made progressive measures in the late 1990s to enhance air quality in the member countries. The EU first adopted its Directive on Ambient Air Quality Assessment and Management in 1996, and another in 1997, aimed at providing reciprocal information exchange between networks and individual monitoring stations. These efforts were realized in 1999 by adopting a directive that sought to set out air quality standards and related guidelines for member states. This directive focused on the following pollutants: sulphur dioxide, nitrogen dioxide, oxides of nitrogen, PM, and lead. Subsequent directives issued by the European Parliament and Council expanded upon these standards, with the directive in 2000 addressing limit values for benzene and CO, and the directive in 2002 focusing on limit values for ozone. In 2004, the directive relating to arsenic, cadmium, mercury, nickel, and polycyclic aromatic hydrocarbons in ambient air was undertaken (European Parliament, Council of the European Union, 2004).

Based on these premises, Directive 2008/50/EC of the European Parliament and the Council (European Parliament, Council of the European Union, 2008) went even further by establishing challenging goals for improving human health and the environment until 2020. This directive combined previous legislation on air quality into one piece, making the regulatory processes less complicated and encouraging cooperation between the member states. It also incorporated WHO guidelines and programs to make sure that it has complete regulatory coverage. In general, the directives focused on 12 air pollutants: arsenic, benzene, benzo(a)pyrene, cadmium, CO, lead, nickel, nitrogen dioxide/NO$_x$, ozone, sulphur dioxide, and PM (PM$_{2.5}$, PM$_{10}$). The directives also set the thresholds, limit values, and target values of each pollutant for the evaluation of air quality. Thresholds are defined as levels of concentrations of pollutants that can potentially have adverse effects on human health or the environment. The limit values define the maximum allowable concentrations of pollutants that should not be exceeded, while the target values are the concentrations of pollutants that should ideally be achieved.

According to the directives, member states are required to develop air quality plans or measures where the concentration of pollutants exceeds the limit or target values. These plans are drawn to identify the sources of pollution and the measures to be taken to reduce their effects with special reference to the sensitive population including children and the elderly. Measures may include applying emission standards, regulating traffic flow, and promoting the use of environmentally friendly technologies. National authorities are required to appoint specific entities to perform these duties using data collected from specified sampling sites. Moreover, the directives stress the need to involve the public in the formulation and execution of air quality policies and measures. National authorities are responsible for providing air quality information (including current data on pollutants and their impact on human health) to the public, environmental NGOs, healthcare institutions, and industrial associations. This makes the process transparent and encourages cooperation in dealing with the problems of air quality on the local, national, and EU levels. Where negligence leads to violation of provisions of the EU air quality standards, national courts have the jurisdiction to handle such cases as seen in many decisions in several member states.

The directive also requires member states to establish robust air quality monitoring networks to assess the levels of pollutants in ambient air and routinely report air quality data to the European Commission. These rules require the creation of a comprehensive air quality monitoring network of over 4,000 monitoring stations strategically placed in urban, industrial, and rural areas across the EU. These monitoring stations gather information on a range of air pollutants, allowing member states to evaluate whether established standards are being met and, if not, to take the necessary corrective action.

The Clean Air Program for Europe was proposed in 2013 by the European Commission (2013b). This extensive legislative package sought to address many areas of air quality management, building on earlier directives and initiatives. Its main goals were to set more ambitious targets, enhance monitoring and reporting systems, and encourage the adoption of cleaner technologies and practices. It included two legislative measures: a directive to minimize pollution from medium-sized combustion installations and a revised National Emissions Ceilings Directive with emission reduction targets for 2020 and 2030.

In the short term, the Programme sought to confront existing challenges, as over a third of EU Air Quality Management Zones exceeded the limit values for PM (PM_{10}), and a quarter exceeded limits for nitrogen dioxide. In response, infringement proceedings were initiated against 17 member states for PM_{10} non-compliance. The main effort was to ensure the full implementation of existing air quality standards by 2020 and enable the effective operation of complementary national measures.

Looking forward, the Programme established new 2030 objectives and identified concrete measures for achieving them. For example, it identified the need for revising emission directives and further improving source controls, especially about ammonia emissions from agriculture. On top of that, it looked at the potential economic benefits and global market opportunities brought by policies for cleaner air. It underlined that cleaner air policies are conducive to growth by improving labour productivity and opening up new business opportunities for European firms in the rapidly expanding global market in environmental technologies and services. It, thus, included incentives to use cleaner technologies and practices in, for example, transport, energy production, and industry. It proposed measures for low-emission vehicles, transition to renewable energy sources, and use of emission reduction technologies in industrial plants, among other things. In so doing, the Programme stressed how European businesses can win a competitive edge by capitalizing on the growing global demand for clean air solutions and thereby, contribute to solving the problem of air pollution worldwide. Again, environmental protection had to be based on both health and economic arguments to make Europe more competitive.

Progress was to be checked every five years, with the first review in 2020. The European Clean Air Forum was established to coordinate implementation and stakeholder engagement, including transparency and accountability in the achievement of the Programme's objectives. One other important aspect of the Programme was revising and strengthening EU air quality standards to take up-to-date science and evolving health risks associated with air pollution. For example, the package aimed at tightening limits on key pollutants such as PM, nitrogen dioxide, sulphur dioxide, ozone, and VOC. It was by laying down stricter standards that the European Commission sought to protect, more effectively.

In addition to revising standards, the package also emphasized the importance of improving monitoring and reporting capabilities. These included remote sensing and satellite monitoring to complement traditional ground monitoring stations. Improving the availability and reliability of air quality data helped policymakers, stakeholders and the public make more informed decisions. In addition, the EU has proposed new CO_2 emission standards for cars and vans to encourage innovation and increase the supply of low- and zero-emission vehicles on the market. Additionally, norms were implemented to protect worker health and safety, including setting minimum requirements for workplace air quality and setting limits on exposure to hazardous substances in the workplace.

In the general picture, the EU legislation represented a comprehensive and forward-looking strategy to tackle air pollution on the continent. It combined stricter standards, enhanced monitoring capabilities, and targeted measures to promote cleaner technologies and practices. It mostly focused on emission thresholds for vehicles (EURO standards) and non-road mobile machinery, as well as criteria for energy efficiency, industrial emissions, product efficiency (under the eco-design directive), and fuel standards. This includes regulations on the sulphur content of specific liquid fuels, primarily targeting SO_x emissions from maritime transport, and the Fuel Quality Directive, which addresses air pollution from road transport by setting supplementary fuel quality criteria.

2.3 The Green Deal and emissions – goals versus actions

Despite the above-described ambitious targets, the air quality in many parts of Europe was far from satisfactory. Estimates indicated approximately 400,000 premature deaths annually due to air pollution in Europe. Eutrophication limits were exceeded in 62% of ecosystem areas and 73% of Natura 2000 sites across the EU territory. Air quality constituted a significant concern for EU citizens, with nearly half of respondents in a Eurobarometer survey identifying "air pollution" as one of the top two environmental issues, alongside climate change (European Commission, 2019a). Moreover, the temporary improvement in air quality observed in some areas due to measures taken during the COVID-19 pandemic caught the public's attention to the problem of an unhealthy environment.

Furthermore, an analysis conducted by the European Commission in 2019 revealed that air quality standards within the EU played a critical role in addressing pollution, albeit with only partial effectiveness. Despite their importance, current EU standards fell short of the recommendations provided by scientific advice, suggesting the need for more ambitious targets to adequately address air quality concerns. Among the various types of air quality standards, limit values have proven to be more effective in driving tangible improvements. Other forms of standards, like exposure reduction targets or target values, could mostly complement binding limit values. Moreover, legal enforcement actions taken by the European Commission, coupled with civil society initiatives, have demonstrated effectiveness in ensuring compliance and driving progress towards cleaner air. In conclusion, while air quality standards were a significant step in pollution reduction efforts, there was room for improvement in their stringency and enforcement mechanisms to achieve more substantial and lasting results (European Commission, 2019b).

In 2019, the European Green Deal laid out ambitious objectives of the EU aimed at cutting GHG emissions, enhancing air quality, and transitioning to a carbon-neutral economy by 2050. The overreaching goal is to achieve zero pollution by 2050 and create an environment free of harmful substances. Still, it is evident that effective clean air policy requires a systemic and integrated approach, which incorporates other environmental strategies in relevant policy areas, and the Green Deal with all its actions could be used as a means to strengthen existing efforts. The areas that overlap are manifold and include climate legislation, industry, energy, transport, and agriculture or circular economy. Without mutual consistency, implementing air quality standards may become more expensive, troublesome for both member states and local authorities, and in the end, ineffective.

To align the efforts of various EU policies, the European Commission adopted the Zero Pollution Action Plan in 2021 (European Commission, 2021a). This plan sets ambitious targets, including reducing the health impacts of air pollution by over 55% and decreasing the EU ecosystems affected by air pollution threatening biodiversity by 25% by 2030. Key actions outlined in the plan include revising the Ambient Air Quality Directives, updating EU or international regulatory frameworks to reduce air and noise emissions from transport at the source, and establishing the Zero Pollution Stakeholder Platform, which includes thematic hubs. These ambitions were further strengthened by the new World Health Organization's "Air Quality Guidelines" for PM ($PM_{2.5}$ and PM_{10}), ozone, nitrogen dioxide, sulphur dioxide, and CO being published in September 2021.

A fitness check of the Ambient Air Quality Directives (European Commission, 2021b) showed that the EU air quality standards for several pollutants fall short of the more stringent recommendations outlined in WHO guidelines. Levels lower than those set by the EU were necessary to fill a significant gap in ambition, notably for $PM_{2.5}$, where the existing EU limit value exceeded even the previous WHO guideline from 2005 by a factor of 2.5. Moreover, some part of harmful pollutants like ultrafine particles, black carbon, various metals, and ammonia were still not regulated by the EU legislation.

As there was a need to close the gaps in regulations on emission sources, a similar situation concerned certain sectors. Automotive brake and tire wear in road transport, construction sites that fall outside the scope of the Non-Road Mobile Machinery regulations, non-sulphur emissions by ships and shoreside electrical power, and mobile refrigeration units still needed legal frames. There was also an appending need to better support local authorities in air quality monitoring, modelling, and plans. It was estimated that the air quality monitoring network across the EU worked effectively and provided reliable and representative air quality measurements and data. Still, some considerations, expressed by various stakeholders as well as the European Court of Auditors, remained whether sampling points accurately capture both the areas with the highest concentrations of pollutants and those representative of general population exposure. Additionally, the absence of standardized modelling practices impeded collaborative scientific efforts. Concerns regarding data comparability across various locations, particularly for pollutants such as nitrogen dioxide, raised worries about the potential underestimation of air pollution levels due to inadequate monitoring in certain areas. A possible solution could be the introduction of new digital tools, also in real-time, and the increased use of lower-cost sensors and open data. These could improve the process of monitoring but also general public awareness and initiate new initiatives including business solutions. There was also a pending need to include air protection goals in sectoral initiatives under the European Green Deal, such as energy production, renewable energy, residential heating, smart mobility, smart sector integration, renovation of buildings, agriculture, and industry. The examples in transport include a faster switch to low- and zero-emission vehicles (phase-out plans for the most polluting vehicles in urban areas across the EU); prioritizing public transport infrastructure, promotion of active mobility, and reconsidering the model of "smart working" changing post-COVID urban mobility transport needs.

Moreover, there was a necessity to reformulate the Common Agriculture Policy (CAP) in the upcoming programming period. While the first pillar (direct subsidies to the farmers) encompassed initiatives aimed at decreasing ammonium emissions, and the second pillar (rural development policy) offered funding avenues for executing air quality initiatives, the emphasis on air quality remained somewhat limited. It became imperative to encourage the adoption of renewable energy sources with minimal air quality repercussions, while also carefully considering the equilibrium between land use and soil utilization for agricultural activities. Similarly, air protection was to be incorporated into the Farm to Fork strategy.

Finally, the governance structure of the Air Quality Directives called for remodelling mainly at the national level. Responsibility for compliance with limit values set by the directives as well as implementation actions was often ceded to local authorities (mostly in urban areas). As a result, a significant portion of emission sources contributing to elevated local concentrations of pollutants often fell beyond the jurisdiction of the responsible entity. While emission source legislation, such as regulations for vehicles or industrial installations, has increasingly been adopted and harmonized at the EU level, local authorities were often left with limited tools to address air quality issues directly. These tools may include measures like driving bans or restrictions on the use of solid fuel installations in private households. Heavy pressure was put on cities in the last few years, which was even more visible after the outbreak of the COVID-19 pandemic, and the Russian attack on Ukraine highlighted the need for greater local participation at all levels of governance. The quest for bigger autonomy and inclusiveness of different stakeholders expanded and must have been acknowledged by national governments, which should express new ambitions and reflect them in both the national air pollution control programs (NAPCPs) and the national energy and climate plans (NECPs).

As a result of rising ambitions generated by the Green Deal, as well as stronger pressure from the civil society, the European Commission proposed the revision of the Ambient Air Quality Directives on 26th of October, 2022 (European Commission, 2022b). The proposals represented a significant advancement for the European Green Deal's ambition to achieve the Zero Pollution Action Plan by 2050 and responded to specific demands raised during the Conference on the Future of Europe. The process of consultations and building political support was challenging and took one year and a half before the agreement between the European Parliament and the Council was reached (European Commission, 2024).

The proposed revision primarily aims to align with the new WHO limits by targeting reductions in PM and nitrogen dioxide levels. For example, the proposal includes a significant decrease in annual mean $PM_{2.5}$ and PM_{10} concentrations. The proposed $PM_{2.5}$ concentration limit will decrease by more than 100% from 25 µg/m³ to 10 µg/ m³, while the PM_{10} threshold limit will be tightened by 100% from 40 *µg/m³ to* 20 *µg/ m³*. Additionally, the annual concentration limit for nitrogen dioxide will be reduced from 40 µg/ m³ to 20 µg/ m³ (Table 2.1).

National and local authorities will develop tailor-made measures to meet these standards, reinforced by existing and new EU policies covering environment, energy, transport, agriculture, research, and innovation. Moreover, the change gave people affected by health problems resulting from air pollution the right to compensation in the event of breaches of EU air quality rules, while increasing the transparency of legal remedies, imposing effective penalties, and increasing public awareness of air quality issues. Citizens will also have the right to be represented by non-governmental organizations (NGOs) in collective actions for damages. In addition, the proposal strengthened local authorities by improving provisions on air quality monitoring and modelling, thereby improving air quality plans. These improvements will facilitate more accurate control of compliance with standards and enable more efficient and

Table 2.1 Air pollution norms of the European Union and the World Health Organization

Parameter	Time Interval	EU 2008	EU 2024 Proposal	WHO 2005	WHO 2021
$PM_{2.5}$	Annual mean	25 µg/m3	10 µg/m3	10 µg/m3	5 µg/m3
	24-hour mean	NA	25 µg/m3	25 µg/m3	15 µg/m3
PM_{10}	Annual mean	40 µg/m3	20 µg/m3	20 µg/m3	15 µg/m3
	24-hour mean	50 µg/m3 Not to be exceeded on more than 35 days/year	45 µg/m3 Not to be exceeded on more than 18 days/year	50 µg/m3	45 µg/m3
NO_2	Annual mean	40 µg/m3	20 µg/m3	40 µg/m3	10 µg/m3
	1-hour mean	200 µg/m3 Not to be exceeded on more than 18 hours/year	200 µg/m3 Not to be exceeded on more than 18 hours/year	NA µg/m3	NA µg/m3
	24-hour mean	NA	50 µg/m3 Not to be exceeded on more than 35 days/year	NA µg/m3	25 µg/m3
O_3	8-hour mean	120 µg/m3 Not to be exceeded on more than 25 days/year	120 µg/m3 Not to be exceeded on more than 18 days/year	100 µg/m3	100 µg/m3

Source: Own study based on the data from the European Parliament, Council of the European Union (2008); European Commission (2024); World Health Organization (2005, 2021)

effective actions to prevent and remediate violations. In addition, the revised directive made it mandatory to take early action to achieve cleaner air. If, in the meantime, pollution levels exceed the new 2030 standards, member states must assess their progress towards compliance and implement the necessary measures to ensure compliance by 2030, with possible extensions subject to rigorous justifications based on careful analysis. Ultimately, member states must undertake appropriate measures to promptly meet air quality standards. The proposal put forward projected gross annual benefits from €42 billion to €121 billion by 2030, at an annual cost of less than €6 billion (European Commission, 2022b).

Altogether, the Green Deal addressed many challenges connected with air pollution. First, the legislative framework has been updated to the current needs, or rather politically achievable levels. The degree of aspiration may be considered as higher than in the pre-2020 period, as it encompasses higher norms, incorporates more sectors, and gives more impetus to national authorities but still not fully satisfactory as norms for most pollutants do not match with WHO standards.

2.4 European attitudes towards air quality

In recent years, there has been a growing public focus on air pollution and its impact on human well-being. Smog alerts, breathing problems, levels of PM, or materials used to heat homes have become permanent elements of discourse in many countries, and families. The awareness of the damaging effects of air pollutants on health has visibly increased, making individuals recognize their role as consumers, residents, and voters. Simultaneously, the function of environmental NGOs, both international and local, changed from protests to education campaigns and legal action against authorities. However, despite these positive developments, governments are failing to prioritize public health over immediate economic benefits, both large and small companies are prioritizing financial gains, and there remains a persistent lack of awareness about scientific evidence (Client Earth, 2015).

Many factors, including perceptions of the efficiency of public policies, influence an individual's air quality attitudes. When people believe they cannot trust risk managers or authorities, they tend to perceive higher risks. The most dependable stakeholders, however, appear to be NGOs and scientists. Also, personal characteristics (age, sex, and education), beliefs and experiences (one's residence, health issues), and broader value orientations can change the perception of air quality. Furthermore, media coverage plays a significant role in shaping environmental communication. Besides traditional mass media, social media activism gained momentum, which proved to be effective in countries like Poland and Great Britain (Grossberndt et al., 2020, p. 23). It is also the current social and political situation, both on a global and regional scale, that can moderate the perception of the importance of environmental issues. Recent game-changers, such as the COVID-19 pandemic and the war in Ukraine, have temporarily frozen the eminence of air pollution for many European citizens, but on the other hand, from a longer perspective, they proved that the green shift is imminent.

As a result, according to the Eurobarometer 2023, the top three problems for EU citizens were poverty, hunger, and lack of drinking water (20%), armed conflict (19%), and climate change (17%). The survey mirrored the lack of political and economic stability caused by the Russian invasion of Ukraine in February 2022, in comparison to the Eurobarometer from 2021, which better reflected the health effects of COVID-19. This geopolitical shift may explain why perceptions of climate change have dropped from first to third place as the most important issue facing the EU. World population growth (7%) followed the economic situation (11%) and retained fourth position. Health problems due to pollution were considered the least important challenge out of 11, which also included the proliferation of nuclear weapons, the deterioration of nature, the deterioration of democracy and rule of law, international terrorism, and the spread of infectious diseases (European Commission, 2023, p. 10).

In the case of air pollution perceptions, they must be analysed more like a trend than a short-term situation. The results of a comparative analysis covering three Eurobarometer surveys from 2012, 2019, and 2022 indicate that there is a growing tendency to perceive the deterioration in air quality – an increase from 56% in 2012 to 75% in 2022 (European Commission, 2013a, 2019a, 2022a). The majority of EU citizens (59%, 54%, *and* 59%) have expressed a sense of inadequate information about air quality issues in their respective countries. Only one-third have heard of the EU air quality standards, but 67% of those who were aware of them advocated for their strengthening.

In 2019, respondents asked about the actors who, they think, have not done enough to promote good air quality and indicated mostly public authorities (66%), energy producers (65%), car manufacturers (64%), households (52%), and farmers (49%). In 2022, the main responsibility shifted to large industrial installations (73%), energy producers (65%), and the government (60%). In three countries, respondents felt particularly disappointed with their government's actions: Greece (81%), Croatia (80%), and the Netherlands (78%). Compared to 2019, the general tendency also prevails to take responsibility from individual households, with the sharpest increases in Greece, Austria, Sweden, and Poland.

All three Eurobarometer surveys asked about personal input to reduce harmful emissions. In 2022, 40% claimed they had replaced old energy-intensive equipment with newer equipment with a better energy rating, a visible drop from 54% in 2012 but comparable to 41% in 2019. Respectively, 63% *vs.* 35% *vs.* 41% have frequently used public transport, bicycles, or walking instead of choosing the car. In 2012, only almost one-tenth (9%) claimed to have not done anything; however, in 2019, this trend amounted to 28%, fortunately dropping to 20% in 2022.

According to the majority of respondents, the most effective way to tackle air pollution was through stricter pollution controls on industrial and energy production activities, reaching more than 40% of answers (43% *vs* 44% *vs* 36%). The second most popular solution in 2022 was encouraging low-emission transport modes (30%) and introducing penalties (26%). Providing higher financial incentives for low-emission products became popular: it amounted to 35% in 2012, 27% in 2019, and dropped to 22% in 2022. Making air quality legislation stricter was mentioned by 18% in 2022 versus 27% in 2019. As a result of ongoing actions to control vehicle emissions, support for this solution dropped from 27% in 2012 to 25% in 2019, reaching only 13% in 2022. Other answers included better enforcement of existing legislation, providing more information to the public about health and environmental consequences, and increasing taxation on air-polluting activities. Surprisingly, only 5 in 100 Europeans wanted improved citizens' access to courts to guarantee clean air in 2022.

The preferred level of action for addressing air pollution remained international, though it decreased from 72% in 2019 to 65% in 2022. This was still the most mentioned answer in 23 countries. In contrast, the national level was the top choice in Ireland (53%), Romania (50%), and Bulgaria (49%), averaging 42% overall, similar to the EU level. Only about one-third of respondents felt that local and regional officials should handle air pollution. A holistic approach involving all levels was most popular in Sweden (33%), Slovenia (30%), and Germany (28%), but least favoured in Bulgaria, Czechia, Greece, Malta, Romania, and Spain.

In the case of climate change, general attitudes moved towards a faster carbon-free transition, which was the reflection of advancements within Green Deal policies but also war-induced repercussions of energy gas supply disturbances and price spikes. Consequently, according to the Eurobarometer from May 2023–June 2023 (European Commission, 2023) for more than three-quarters (77%) of EU citizens, climate change became a very serious problem. Respondents in seven countries considered climate change to be the world's most serious problem: Belgium, Denmark, Germany, Ireland, Malta, the Netherlands, Austria, Finland, and Sweden. In 16 countries, climate change ranked in the top three. The majority of Europeans believed that the EU (56%), national governments (56%), businesses (53%), and regional and local authorities (36%) were responsible for solving the problem. Only 35% felt personally responsible, but still, six in ten citizens said they had taken action over the last six months. More than eight in ten respondents were convinced that their national governments (86%) and the EU (85%) must take action to improve energy efficiency by 2030. However, only 23% of respondents believed that national governments had done enough, while 5% claimed they had done too much.

Most Europeans trusted that the transition to a green economy should be accelerated. Given the rising energy prices and Russian measures to restrict natural gas supply, 58% of respondents advocated for accelerating the use of renewable energy, improving energy efficiency, and accelerating the transition to a green economy. 25% of respondents advocated for maintaining the pace of transformation, while 12% thought that more fossil fuels should be used during the energy crisis and that the transition to a green economy should be slowed down. Three-quarters of respondents (75%) had confidence that action on climate change will lead to innovation and make EU businesses more competitive (29% strongly agree, 46% partially agree). Nearly as many people (73%) agreed that the costs of damage caused by climate change are much higher than the costs of investing in a green transition (33% strongly agree, 40% partially agree). The majority (84%) also believed that climate change and environmental issues should be a priority to improve public health. Seven in ten respondents (70%) approved that the reduction of fossil fuel imports from outside the EU would improve energy security and bring economic benefits to the EU (27% strongly agree, 43% partially agree).

To alleviate the economic pressure caused by the energy crisis, the preferred course of action was to accelerate the development of renewable energy (29%) and adopt economic measures (29%). This was followed by direct financial support (16%) and increased investment in energy efficiency measures (15%). Notably, the least chosen option was the diversification of EU fossil fuel import supplies (6%). Nearly eight in ten respondents agreed that the clean energy transition should receive greater public financial support, even if it means reducing fossil fuel subsidies (36% strongly agree, 42% tend to agree).

The above-described attitudes are to a high extent a result of the rising level of environmental awareness and participation of European citizens. Free and unrestricted access to information is a legal right for all citizens of EU member states. Citizens now have the right to access national air quality plans and data on air quality at their request. The European Commission and the general public must receive information on the implementation of Ambient Air Quality Directives from member states. Despite the right to access information, Europeans are eligible to participate in the formulation of plans relating to the environment and to access courts to challenge breaches of environmental law. It is the responsibility of national authorities to make sure that the public is informed about air quality in a timely and sufficient manner, particularly when thresholds are exceeded.

Starting from 1989, the EU is also a party to an international treaty – the "Aarhus Convention" from 1998 claiming that "Every person has the right to live in an environment adequate to his or her health and well-being, and the duty, both individually and in association with others, to protect and improve the environment for the benefit of present and future generations" (UNECE, 1998, p. 2). In October 2021, the amended Aarhus Regulation was adopted by the European Parliament (2021), broadening access to information, public participation in decision-making, and access to justice in environmental matters. The new regulations were thought to bring more effective penalties and compensation possibilities for violating air quality rules, as well as improved public information.

However, the existing legislation does not incorporate provisions that allow individuals to seek reparation for health-related harm resulting from air pollution. The European Court of Justice (ECJ) has issued several significant judgments regarding the legal interpretation and impact of limit values. These legal decisions have established the principle that individuals possess a legal entitlement to breathe unpolluted air under European Union legislation. The Court has consistently ruled that limited values grant specific rights to citizens of the European Union, which can be enforced in national courts. As a result, in 2024, there were 53 legal cases against member states being led by the ClientEarth watchdog organization against such countries as Belgium, Bulgaria, France, Germany, Hungary, Italy, the Netherlands, Poland, Romania, and the UK (Politico, 2024).

Independently, the European Commission can step up its enforcement against member states for failing to comply with the norms. In 2024, there were 59 ongoing infringement cases against EU member countries including Poland, Italy, Bulgaria, Romania, and Portugal among the top offenders. In fact, only three countries not facing legal proceedings were the Netherlands, Slovakia, and Estonia (Politico, 2024). Similar cases also include suits against ineptitude and procrastination of national governments in the area of climate protection. On 24th of April, 2024, the European Court of Human Rights in the case brought by the Swiss Elders for Climate Protection undertook the landmark decision that the government's inaction on climate change violates fundamental human rights. This ruling was perceived as a breaking point as similar cases of Portuguese youth (Voza et al., 2022) and a former French mayor were turned by the judges (Euronews, 2024).

Besides legal actions, which are still the most radical and final form of activism, no matter if initiated by the European institutions, or average citizens, air pollution control and management also has been involving the growing amount of participatory actions. First, in 2017, the European Commission initiated the "Clean Air Dialogues" with a willingness to cooperate with member states. Till 2021, they were conducted with eight countries. Also, during the Conference on the Future of Europe in 2021, citizens participated in Panel 3 dedicated to climate change and the environment and health. As a part of the Green Deal revision in the area of air pollution, the EU organized a series of consultations with NGOs, which resulted in valuable recommendations. Moreover, the EU Clean Air Forum has become a meeting point for decision-makers from European, national, and local levels, along with various stakeholders like business and industry, NGOs, academia, and experts from across society.

Recent years have also brought a visible rise in the significance of metropolitan areas, as the level of governance that is nearest to citizens. They play a vital role in not only carrying out measures to reduce pollution but also in supplying air quality data and engaging citizens in the creation of these measures Due to heightened citizen awareness in recent decades, the advent of new technologies (including smartphone apps) and real-time data for monitoring air quality (Air Quality Index, 2024), there has been a proliferation of citizen-initiated activities that offer valuable information. They were presented by the European Environment Agency (2013, 2018) in the form of the so-called Air Implementation Pilot and reports on citizen science (European Environment Agency, 2019). Low-carbon economy transition and resilience at the urban level are also key priorities among city organizations like Eurocities, NetZero Cities, and Covenant of Mayors. These bodies permanently share knowledge and experiences promoting solution-based, practical approaches.

Summing up, the level of awareness and participation is steadily increasing as a result of improved information distribution, enhanced networking, and the proactive involvement of local authorities. Due to increased access to information, citizens are now more knowledgeable, resulting in higher levels of engagement in efforts to enhance air quality. The continuous upward trajectory of this positive trend suggests that in the future, air quality concerns will be addressed through well-informed and collaborative efforts across all sectors of society.

Reference list

Air Quality Index. (2024). https://www.eea.europa.eu/themes/air/air-quality-index.

Chivian, E., McCally, M., Hu, H., & Haines, A. (1993). *Critical condition: Human health and the environment*. The MIT Press.

Client Earth. (2015). *Clean air handbook. A practical guide to EU air quality law. Version 2.0*. https://www.clientearth.org/media/aeph4gln/2015-11-30-clean-air-handbook-version-two-ce-en.pdf

Euronews. (2024, April 9). *Historic European Court of Human Rights ruling backs Swiss women in climate change case*. https://www.euronews.com/green/2024/04/09/top-european-human-rights-court-could-rule-that-governments-have-to-protect-people-from-cl

European Commission. (2013a). *Attitudes of Europeans towards air quality*. Flash Eurobarometer 360. https://europa.eu/eurobarometer/surveys/detail/2660

European Commission. (2013b). *Communication from the commission to the European Parliament, the Council, the European Economic and Social Committee and the Committee of the Regions: A clean air programme for Europe (COM/2013/0918 final)*. https://eur-lex.europa.eu/LexUriServ/LexUriServ.do?uri=COM%3A2013%3A0918%3AFIN%3AEN%3APDF

European Commission. (2018). *Communication from the commission to the European Parliament, the Council, the European Economic and Social Committee and the Committee of the Regions a Europe that protects: Clean air for all (COM/2018/330 final)*. https://eur-lex.europa.eu/legal-content/EN/TXT/PDF/?uri=CELEX:52018DC0330

European Commission. (2019a). *Attitudes of Europeans towards air quality*. Special Eurobarometer 497. https://europa.eu/eurobarometer/surveys/detail/2239

European Commission. (2019b). *Commission staff working document fitness check of the ambient air quality directives. SWD(2019) 427 final*. https://commission.europa.eu/document/download/096e018e-725c-4a17-9227-0c01f4b38031_en?filename=swd_2019_0427_en.pdf&prefLang=pl

European Commission. (2021a). *Communication from the commission to the European Parliament, the Council, the European Economic and Social Committee and the Committee of the Regions Pathway to a Healthy Planet for All. EU action plan: 'Towards zero pollution for air, water and soil'*. Com/2021/400Final.https://eur-lex.europa.eu/legal-content/EN/ALL/?uri=COM%3A2021%3A400%3AFIN

European Commission. (2021b). *Fitness check of the ambient air quality directives. Fit for future platform opinion.* https://commission.europa.eu/document/download/0f239b9d-2ad6-4879-ac99-881b2b1f20e3_en?filename=Final%20opinion%202021_SBGR1_04%20Ambient%20air%20quality_fup_0.pdf&prefLang=pl

European Commission. (2022a). *Attitudes of Europeans towards air quality.* Special Eurobarometer 524. https://europa.eu/eurobarometer/surveys/detail/2660

European Commission. (2022b). *European Green Deal: Commission proposes rules for cleaner air and water.* Press release, Brussels. Retrieved October 26, 2022, from https://ec.europa.eu/commission/presscorner/detail/en/ip_22_6278

European Commission. (2023). *Climate change – report.* Special Eurobarometer 538. https://europa.eu/eurobarometer/surveys/detail/2954

European Commission. (2024). *Commission welcomes provisional agreement for cleaner air in the EU.* Press release, Brussels. Retrieved February 20, 2024, from https://ec.europa.eu/commission/presscorner/detail/en/ip_24_886

European Environment Agency. (2007). *Air pollution in Europe 1990–2004. EEA Report, 2.* https://www.eea.europa.eu/publications/eea_report_2007_2

European Environment Agency. (2013). *Air implementation pilot. Lessons learned from the implementation of air quality legislation at urban level. EEA Report, 7.* https://eea.europa.eu/publications/air-implementation-pilot-2013

European Environment Agency. (2018). *Europe's urban air quality – Re-assessing implementation challenges in cities. EEA Report, 24.* https://www.eea.europa.eu/publications/europes-urban-air-quality

European Environment Agency. (2019). *Assessing air quality through citizen science. EEA Report, 19.* https://www.eea.europa.eu/publications/assessing-air-quality-through-citizen-science

European Environment Agency. (2023). *National air pollutant emissions data viewer 2005–2021.* https://www.eea.europa.eu/data-and-maps/dashboards/necd-directive-data-viewer-7

European Parliament. (2021). *Regulation (EU) 2021/1767 of the European Parliament and of the Council of 6 October 2021 amending regulation (EC) No 1367/2006 on the application of the provisions of the Aarhus convention on access to information, public participation in decision-making and access to justice in environmental matters to community institutions and bodies.* PE/63/2021/REV/1. https://eur-lex.europa.eu/legal-content/EN/TXT/?uri=celex%3A32021R1767

European Parliament, Council of the European Union. (2004). *Directive 2004/107/EC of the European Parliament and of the Council of 15 December 2004 relating to arsenic, cadmium, mercury, nickel and polycyclic aromatic hydrocarbons in ambient air.* Official Journal of the European Union, L 23/3.

European Parliament, Council of the European Union. (2008). *Directive 2008/50/EC of the European Parliament and of the Council of 21 May 2008 on ambient air quality and cleaner air for Europe.* Official Journal of the European Union, L 152/1.

52   *Katarzyna Dośpiał-Borysiak*

European Parliament, Council of the European Union. (2013). *Decision No 1386/2013/EU of the European Parliament and of the Council of 20 November 2013 on a general union environment action programme to 2020 'Living well, within the limits of our planet' Text with EEA relevance*. Official Journal of the European Union, L 354/171. https://eur-lex.europa.eu/legal-content/EN/TXT/?uri=CELEX:32013D1386

European Parliament, Council of the European Union. (2016). *Directive (EU) 2016/2284 of the European Parliament and of the Council of 14 December 2016 on the reduction of national emissions of certain atmospheric pollutants, amending Directive 2003/35/EC and repealing Directive 2001/81/EC (Text with EEA relevance)*. https://eur-lex.europa.eu/legal-content/EN/TXT/?uri=uriserv%3AOJ.L_.2016.344.01.0001.01.ENG

Fowler, D., Brimblecombe, P., Burrows, J., Heal, M., Grennfelt, P., Stevenson, D., Jowett, A., Nemitz, E., Coyle, M., Liu, X., Chang, Y., Fuller, G., Sutton, M., Klimont, Z., Unsworth, M., & Vieno, M. (2020). A chronology of global air quality. *Philosophical Transactions. Series A, Mathematical, Physical, and Engineering Sciences, 378*(2183), 20190314.

Grossberndt, S., Bartonova, A., & Ortiz, A. (2020). Public awareness and efforts to improve air quality in Europe. *Eionet Report – ETC/ATNI, 2*.

Hoesly, R. M., Smith, S. J., Feng, L., Klimont, Z., Janssens-Maenhout, G., Pitkanen, T., Seibert, J. J., Vu, L., Andres, R. J., Bolt, R. M., Bond, T. C., Dawidowski, L., Kholod, N., Kurokawa, J.-I., Li, M., Liu, L., Lu, Z., Moura, M. C. P., O'Rourke, P. R., & Zhang, Q. (2018). Historical (1750–2014) anthropogenic emissions of reactive gases and aerosols from the Community Emissions Data System (CEDS). *Geoscientific Model Development, 11*(1), 369–408. https://doi.org/10.5194/gmd-11-369-2018

Igini, M. (2022, October 23). Air pollution: Have we reached the point of no return? *Earth.org*. https://earth.org/history-of-air-pollution/.

Li, C., van Donkelaar, A., Hammer, M. S., et al. (2023). Reversal of trends in global fine particulate matter air pollution. *Nature Communications, 14*(1), 5349. https://doi.org/10.1038/s41467-023-41086-z

NASA Earth Observatory. (2024). *Ozone*. https://earthobservatory.nasa.gov/world-of-change/Ozone

Politico. (2024). *EU countries demand 10 extra years to meet air pollution targets*. https://www.politico.eu/article/eu-countries-demand-10-extra-years-meet-air-pollution-targets/

Shy, C., Goldsmith, J. R., Hackney, J. D., Lebowitz, M. D., & Menzel, D. B. (1978). *Health effects of air pollution*. New York Lung Association.

UNECE. (1979). *1979 Convention on long-range transboundary air pollution*. https://unece.org/sites/default/files/2021-05/1979%20CLRTAP.e.pdf

UNECE. (1998). *Convention on access to information, public participation in decision-making and access to justice in environmental matters, done at Aarhus, Denmark, on 25 June 1998*. https://unece.org/DAM/env/pp/documents/cep43e.pdf

UNECE. (2016). *Towards cleaner air: Scientific assessment report 2016. EMEP steering body and working group on effects of the convention on long-range transboundary air pollution, Oslo*. https://core.ac.uk/reader/83641740

UNECE. (2018). *Decision 2018/5. Annex. Long-term strategy for the convention on long-range transboundary air pollution for 2020–2030 and beyond.* https://unece.org/fileadmin/DAM/env/documents/2018/Air/EB/correct_numbering_Decision_2018_5.pdf

UNECE. (2024a). *Protocol to abate acidification, eutrophication, and ground-level ozone.* https://unece.org/environment-policy/air/protocol-abate-acidifi cation-eutrophication-and-ground-level-ozone

UNECE. (2024b). *Protocols.* https://unece.org/protocols

Voza, D., Milošević, I., & Vuković, M. (2022). Comparative analysis of environmental attitudes of youth from EU member and candidate states: Case study central and eastern Europe. *TEME: Casopis za Društvene Nauke, 46*(1), 175–193.

World Health Organization. (2005). *Air quality guidelines. Global update 2005. Particulate matter, ozone, nitrogen dioxide and sulfur dioxide.* https://www.who.int/publications/i/item/WHO-SDE-PHE-OEH-06.02

World Health Organization. (2021). *WHO global air quality guidelines: Particulate matter (PM2.5 and PM10), ozone, nitrogen dioxide, sulfur dioxide and carbon monoxide.* https://iris.who.int/bitstream/handle/10665/345329/9789240034228-eng.pdf?sequence=1

3   Trends of air pollution in the European Union – comparative perspective

Magdalena Tomala

Carbon dioxide (CO_2) emissions have played a significant role in the Earth because they are one of the leading causes of climate change. Thanks to climate research, the international community is becoming increasingly aware of the effects of rising temperatures on the planet (Letcher, 2021, p. 4), as well as on essential areas of the environment as sea level rise (Cazenave & Llovel, 2010, pp. 145–173; Swapna et al., 2020, pp. 175–189), the Arctic (Koenigk et al., 2020, pp. 673–705; Łuszczuk, 2011, pp. 93–100; Walsh et al., 2011, pp. 6–16), changes in the vegetation of plants (Lloyd & Farquhar, 2008, pp. 1811–1817), and animals migration (Kubelka et al., 2022, pp. 30–41; Seebacher & Post, 2015, pp. 1–2) etc. There is also a growing understanding of the impact of rising temperatures on human health (Xu et al., 2020, pp. 2173–2181).

Therefore, the European Union's (EU) policy rightly focuses on CO_2 emissions to implement the Green Deal. However, it is crucial to understand the intricate relationship between CO_2 emissions and air pollution. The correlation between greenhouse gas (GHG) emissions and air pollution is not coincidental; it arises from many activities that produce GHGs and release other pollutants into the atmosphere. For instance, the combustion of fossil fuels for energy production releases CO_2 (Sathre, 2014, p. 674), as well as pollutants such as nitrogen oxides (NO_x), sulphur dioxide (SO_2), and particulate matter (PM). (Constantin et al., 2020, pp. 1–2). Industrial processes like manufacturing and refining emit GHGs and various air pollutants. Also, agricultural practices, including livestock farming and fertilizer use, contribute to GHG emissions (Bennetzen et al., 2016, pp. 43–55) (e.g., methane (CH_4) from enteric fermentation and nitrous oxide (N_2O) from soil management) and air pollution (Abbasi et al., 2014, pp. 347–387) (e.g., ammonia emissions) (Sakadevan & Nguyen, 2017, pp. 147–184). Furthermore, some pollutants, such as black carbon (a component of particulate matter), have both climate-warming and air-polluting properties. Figure 3.1 illustrates this complex interdependence.

A correlation coefficient of 0.5 suggests a moderate tendency for air emissions intensities and exposure to air pollution by PM to increase together. In

DOI: 10.4324/9781032707006-4

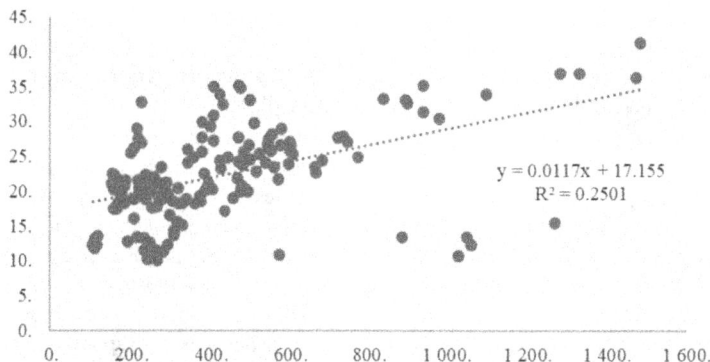

Figure 3.1 Dependency between air emissions intensities and air pollution
Source: Own study based on the data from (Eurostat, 2021, 2023)

other words, as air emissions intensities increase, exposure to air pollution by PM also tends to increase, and vice versa. It suggests that regions or areas with higher air emissions intensities will likely experience higher exposure to particulate matter pollution. This information is valuable for policymakers and environmental authorities in designing strategies to mitigate air pollution and reduce emissions because of consequences for people's health and environmental issues. Countries like Bulgaria, Estonia, Greece, Croatia, Lithuania, and Poland have relatively high emissions intensities as well as high levels of pollution. Conversely, countries like Sweden, Finland, and Ireland have relatively low emissions intensities and low levels of pollution. Some countries have a mix of high or moderate emissions intensities and varying pollution levels. For example, Czechia, Denmark, Germany, Spain, France, Italy, Cyprus, Latvia, Luxembourg, Hungary, the Netherlands, Austria, Portugal, Romania, Slovenia, and Slovakia fall into this category. Targeted efforts to reduce emissions are, therefore, still required to protect human health and the environment in Europe further.

It is worth underlining that both variables are interconnected but represent different aspects of environmental degradation. GHGs such as carbon dioxide (CO_2), CH_4, N_2O, and fluorinated gases trap heat in the Earth's atmosphere, leading to the greenhouse effect (Norby & Luo, 2004, p. 281). Human activities, mainly burning fossil fuels for energy, industrial processes, deforestation, and agricultural practices, contribute to the increase in GHG emissions. These emissions are the primary drivers of climate change, leading to global warming, rising sea levels, extreme weather events, and ecosystem disruptions. Air pollution refers to the presence of harmful or excessive quantities of substances, including pollutants such as PM, NO_x, SO_2, volatile organic compounds (VOCs), and carbon monoxide (CO), in the air. Sources of air pollution include vehicle emissions (Li, 2020, pp. 23–49; Zhang & Batterman, 2013, pp. 307–316), industrial processes (Munsif et al., 2021, pp. 1–14), power generation, agricultural activities, and wildfires.

Moreover, climate change has a detrimental impact on air quality through various mechanisms. First, ozone forms through chemical reactions between NO_x and VOCs in sunlight. Higher temperatures accelerate these reactions, leading to elevated ozone concentrations. Tropospheric ozone harms human health and damages vegetation. Second, photochemical smog is a mixture of air pollutants from sunlight-driven reactions. Warmer temperatures intensify these reactions, worsening photochemical smog. Also, elevated temperatures cause harmful substances like benzene and formaldehyde to evaporate more readily from surfaces, contaminating the air.

Up until roughly a decade ago, air pollution was thought to be merely an urban or localized issue. However, recent data have shown that rapid, long-distance transport carries air pollution across continents and ocean basins, leading to the formation of transoceanic and transcontinental plumes of atmospheric brown clouds (Ramanathan, 2007, p. 473). In addition to increasing temperature, global warming causes changes in atmospheric circulation. Weaker winds and more frequent temperature inversions hinder air pollutant dispersal, leading to their accumulation in the atmosphere. Altered atmospheric circulation patterns can transport air pollutants over vast distances, negatively impacting air quality in regions not responsible for the emissions.

Extreme weather events, once considered infrequent occurrences, are becoming a more frequent and potent consequence of climate change. These events wreak havoc on landscapes and infrastructure and profoundly impact air quality, posing a significant threat to human health. Wildfires are a primary source of air pollution. As these infernos rage, they release vast amounts of smoke and PM into the atmosphere. This PM includes $PM_{2.5}$, fine particles less than 2.5 micrometres in diameter, which can penetrate deep into the lungs, causing respiratory problems, cardiovascular issues, and even premature death. The wildfire smoke also contains harmful gases like CO and ozone, further exacerbating air quality issues (De Sario et al., 2013, pp. 826–843; Tsangari et al., 2016, pp. 247–253).

Droughts, another consequence of climate change, can also lead to declining air quality. When prolonged periods of dry weather deplete water resources, the land becomes parched and susceptible to dust storms. These storms pick up loose soil and organic matter, hurling them into the atmosphere as $PM_{2.5}$ and PM_{10} (particles less than 10 micrometres in diameter). This increase in PM concentration creates a hazy sky and poses health risks similar to wildfire smoke (Johnston et al., 2011, pp. 811–816).

It is worth mentioning that floods, seemingly the opposite of droughts, can also contribute to air pollution. As floodwaters recede, they can trigger soil erosion, releasing harmful substances like heavy metals and other pollutants trapped in the soil. These pollutants can become airborne, further contaminating the air. Additionally, floodwaters can inundate industrial sites and waste disposal facilities, releasing hazardous chemicals into the environment (Fan et al., 2015, pp. 6066–6075; Graham et al., 2022, p. 2246).

In conclusion, extreme weather events, fuelled by climate change, are a growing threat to air quality. Wildfires, droughts, and floods all contribute to increased PM concentrations and the release of harmful pollutants, jeopardizing human health. It is crucial to address the root cause of these events – climate change – through mitigation strategies like reducing GHG emissions and adapting to the changing environment. Only by taking decisive action can countries' governments ensure a future where we – as a society – will breathe clean air, free from the detrimental effects of extreme weather.

Beyond its detrimental effects on human health, climate change also negatively impacts the natural environment. Air pollution can damage plants, animals, and entire ecosystems. Air pollution has numerous adverse effects on human health, including respiratory and cardiovascular diseases, as well as environmental impacts such as acid rain, smog formation, and damage to vegetation.

Available knowledge of the effects of global warming has led international attention to the problem. Nowadays, reducing CO_2 emissions is a crucial challenge for most countries and a significant objective of the EU's long-term strategy. If the EU executes its intentions, it will be carbon neutral by 2050. The actions which the EU has taken are essential for the protection of the environment as well as for future generations. As the European Environment Agency pointed, Europe's air quality has not consistently improved despite the overall reduction in human-caused air pollutant emissions. The reasons for this are multifaceted: a direct linear relationship between lower emissions and observed air pollutant concentrations does not always exist, the increasing contribution of long-distance transport of air pollutants from other countries in the northern hemisphere.

Hence, focused efforts to reduce emissions are still essential to safeguard human health and the environment in Europe and should be carried out with consideration of global warming and human health (European Environment Agency, 2023).

3.1   Key trends of CO_2 emissions and air pollution in the EU countries

International organizations, government agencies, research institutions, and independent climate and environmental monitoring groups systematically study CO_2 emission trends. For instance, the International Energy Agency (IEA) collects and analyses CO_2 emissions data and provides forecasts of global energy consumption and GHG emissions. The 2022 report revealed that global energy-related CO_2 emissions increased by 0.9% or 321 million tonnes, reaching a record high of over 36.8 gigatonnes (International Energy Agency, 2022).

On the other hand, the International Panel on Climate Change (IPCC) is an international scientific body assessing scientific evidence on climate change. It prepares reports based on available data and predicts future trends in CO_2 emissions and their impact on the climate. The IPCC has provided a complete picture of how human-caused climate change affects our plans and how humans can address it (Intergovernmental Panel on Climate Change, 2023).

In addition, national governments worldwide and the EU have gathered and collected studies on CO_2 emissions in their countries. This information is often made publicly available and forms the basis for climate policy. In order to comprehend the actions being undertaken to diminish CO_2 emissions and the challenges yet to be overcome in the context of climate change, it is imperative to conduct research and monitor CO_2 emissions. The aim is to furnish reliable information on which policy decisions and environmental initiatives could be based. International organizations objectively evaluate the trend of CO_2 emissions by utilizing available data on energy production, transport, industry, and other economic sectors.

The EU is one of the world's smaller CO_2 emitters, but it still significantly impacts global warming. China is the largest CO_2 polluter all over the world. In 2022, China's CO_2 emissions were 11.4 billion tonnes, which has increased since the 1990s, but the rate of increase has slowed in recent years. The United States is the second largest CO_2 emitter. In 2022, CO_2 emissions in the United States were 5.06 billion tonnes, twice less than in China. It should be underlined that the United States has been experiencing a decline in smog since 2005. The third largest CO_2 emitter is India, which emitted 2.4 billion tonnes. Similar to China, in India, emissions have been increasing since the 1990s and are expected to continue this trend in the coming years. All 27 countries of the EU have less influence on air quality in the world than the countries mentioned above. However, they still significantly impact global warming and people's health. In 2022, the EU was responsible for 2.76 tonnes of global CO_2 emissions, ranking fourth behind China, the United States and India (Ritchie et al., 2020).

The EU is a leader in the global fight against CO_2 emissions. It has made several ambitious commitments and taken action to decarbonize its economy (see chapter 2). It cannot be ignored that the EU has recently taken a lot of intensive actions to reduce emissions. It should also be remembered that this is not a newly exploded problem. As early as 1992, the need to reduce GHG emissions was established by the United Nations Framework Convention on Climate Change (UNFCCC), and the EU was one of the signatories of this convention. The primary objective of the UNFCCC was to stabilize the concentration of GHGs in the Earth's atmosphere at levels that prevent dangerous human-induced interference with the climate system. The UNFCCC aimed to promote measures to mitigate (reduce) the emissions of GHGs. This included efforts to reduce emissions from energy, transportation, industry, and agriculture sectors. The Convention recognized the need to be adapted to achieve the effects of climate change that are already occurring and those that are expected to happen in the future. The Convention encouraged countries to develop and implement strategies for adapting to changing climatic conditions, especially in vulnerable and developing regions (United Nations, 1992).

It is worth looking at the scale of emissions over a long period to show how significant the air pollution threat is. Before the Industrial Revolution, atmospheric CO_2 had been retained at under 2 t. per capita. From 1850 until the end of WWII, there was an increase of less than 2 t. CO_2 is produced by consuming fossil fuels and by modifying land use. The sum of these emissions rose rapidly after the war, leading to the growth of atmosphere pollution and many other environmental problems. The situation changed in the 1990s and the 20th century, and the trend changed positively. The EU has made progress in reducing CO_2 emissions in recent years. Although the measures taken by the EU are not spectacular, an explicit change of trend appeared in the 1990s. The implication is that the actions taken at the EU level pay several dividends. There is, however, a specific shortfall due to the slight decrease in emissions. It is, therefore, essential to understand why the effects of the measures taken are not satisfactory (Ritchie et al., 2020).

It is worth noting that despite having a common Green Deal strategy, EU countries do not have homogeneous policies. Let us look at European countries' GHG emission trends (see Annexe 3.1). Countries have been divided into three groups: countries with an increasing trend in CO_2 emissions, countries without a trend, and countries with a decreasing trend. Only one country recorded an increasing trend. This is Cyprus, which has specific geographical conditions compared to the other EU countries. It should be noted that the increasing trend in emissions may be influenced in this case by its island location or a small territory (Tomala, 2024, pp. 551–570). A group of 6 of the 27 EU countries (Austria, Croatia, Ireland, Luxembourg, Slovenia, Spain) has no trend, meaning that changes have been so slight over the period under review since 1990 that no change in CO_2 emission parameters can be discerned. In this group, one may also find small countries according to their geographical areas, such as Luxembourg, Slovenia, Croatia, and Austria, and the island's location, such as Ireland. Among the indicated countries, there was a decreasing trend at certain times followed by an increasing trend, or vice versa. Therefore, the linear regression model did not indicate the presence of any trend. Spain, Austria, Ireland, and Croatia, for example, saw increases in CO_2 emissions in the first period, but this has already changed since 2004–2006. By contrast, no significant changes can be observed for Luxembourg and Slovenia. (Annexe 3.1).

These characteristics do not explain the lack of action to improve the level of emissions because, among the EU countries, some, such as Malta, can be identified that, despite their small size, achieve the emission reduction indicated by the EU. Also, economic issues are not as important as political points of view in different countries (Tomala, 2024, pp. 551–570).

The largest group consists of countries that have achieved a positive trend in reducing CO_2 emissions. Here, we deal with 20 countries that meet the EU's Green Deal targets in different ways and speeds. There is no clear answer to the question of the effectiveness of CO_2 emission reductions in individual EU countries, according to various specific factors related to the circumstances of each country.

The data provided reveals a diverse landscape of emission reduction efforts amongst the listed countries between 1992 and 2021 (see: Table 3.1). While several countries achieved impressive progress, with Estonia leading the pack at a remarkable 57.2%decrease, others experienced stagnation or even increases in emissions. Besides Estonia, leaders in emissions reduction are countries such as Denmark, Latvia, Romania, and Sweden, which have

Table 3.1   Decrease in emissions according to specific factors

Ranking	Decrease in emissions between 1992 and 2021 as a percentage	Decrease in emissions as absolute terms	Emission reduction rate as a percentage
1.	Estonia 57.2	Germany 290.8	Estonia 1.91
2.	Denmark 49.3	Italy 110.6	Denmark 1.64
3.	Latvia 48.8	France 100.7	Latvia 1.63
4.	Romania 39.7	Romania 52.2	Romania 1.3
5.	Sweden 37.8	Czechia 48.6	Sweden 1.26
6.	Lithuania 34.5	Poland 36.1	Lithuania 1.15
7.	Greece 33.7	the Netherlands 28.9	Greece 1.12
8.	Czechia 33.3	Denmark 28.8	Czechia 1.11
9.	Luxembourg 31.6	Greece 28.7	Luxembourg 1.05
10.	Finland 30.7	Belgium 26.8	Finland 1.02
11.	Germany 30.12	Sweden 21.8	Germany 1.00
12.	Slovakia 27.7	Finland 16.6	Slovakia 0.92
13.	Bulgaria 25.8	Spain 16.2	Bulgaria 0.86
14.	Italy 25.2	Bulgaria 14.8	Italy 0.84
15.	Malta 24.8	Estonia 13.9	Malta 0.82
16.	France 24.8	Hungary 13.6	France 0.82
17.	Hungary 21.9	Slovakia 13.6	Hungary 0.73
18.	Belgium 21.85	Portugal 10.2	Belgium 0.73
19.	Portugal 19.9	Lithuania 7.3	Portugal 0.66
20.	the Netherlands 17	Latvia 6.9	the Netherlands 0.57
21.	Poland 9.9	Luxembourg 3.8	Poland 0.33
22.	Slovenia 9.6	Slovenia 1.3	Slovenia 0.32
23.	Spain 6.5	Malta 0.5	Spain 0.21
24.	Austria −7.2	Croatia −1.3	Austria −0.24
25.	Croatia −8.1	Cyprus −2.1	Croatia −0.27
26.	Ireland −12.1	Ireland −4.4	Ireland −0.40
27.	Cyprus −37.7	Austria −4.4	Cyprus −1.26

Source: Own study based on the data from Ritchie et al., 2020

stood out as frontrunners, achieving over 35% decrease in emissions. Progress also has been achieved by a significant portion of the countries, including Lithuania, Greece, Czechia, Luxembourg, Finland, Germany, Slovakia, Bulgaria, Italy, Malta, France, Hungary and Belgium, which have exhibited moderate reductions ranging from 20% *to* 35%. Several countries, including Portugal, the Netherlands, Poland, Slovenia, and Spain, displayed minimal progress. On the other hand, there have been negative changes in Austria, Croatia, and Ireland, which shows a need for more substantial efforts. Cyprus exhibited significant increases in emissions, highlighting the complexities and challenges in achieving widespread emission reduction.

While the previous analysis focused on the percentage decrease in emissions, examining the data regarding absolute reduction (million tonnes) reveals a different perspective. For instance, despite a moderate percentage decrease (30.1%), Germany leads in absolute emission reduction with a staggering 290.8 million tonnes due to its large initial emissions footprint. Significant reducers have been Italy, France, Romania, and the Czech Republic following closely, each achieving over 40 million tonnes of absolute reduction. These countries, called moderate reducers, are Poland, the Netherlands, Denmark, Belgium, Sweden, and Greece. They have exhibited reductions between 20 and 40 million tonnes. Low reduction has been achieved by smaller nations like Finland, Spain, Bulgaria, Estonia, Hungary, Slovakia, and Portugal, showcasing reductions between 20 and 10 million tonnes. Stagnation has been observed in Lithuania, Latvia, Luxembourg, Slovenia, and Malta. An increase has displayed negative values, indicating increased total emissions by Austria, Croatia, Ireland, and Cyprus.

This analysis highlights the importance of considering relative and absolute measures when evaluating emission reduction efforts. While some countries have shown impressive progress in percentage decrease, their initial emissions have been high, leading to a lower absolute reduction.

The emission reduction rate offers a valuable metric for understanding the sustained pace at which emissions are declining in a country. While some countries like Estonia, Denmark, Latvia, Romania, Sweden, Lithuania, Greece, Czechia, Luxembourg, Finland, and Germany have achieved improvements, others such as Slovakia, Bulgaria, Italy, Malta, France, Hungary, Belgium, Portugal, the Netherlands, Poland, Slovenia, and Spain, require accelerated efforts to achieve substantial emission reductions. Negative rates highlight the critical need for immediate action in countries experiencing rising emissions, such as Austria, Croatia, Ireland, and Cyprus.

The EU is primarily associated with policies focused on climate change. In the Green Deal document itself, emissions targets come to the fore. However, it should be noted that in the European Commission document itself, which is a kind of strategic declaration, air pollution is one of the main issues to be addressed in the Green Deal. Therefore, in the various reports and analyses on progress towards the EU's climate targets, air pollution is often mentioned

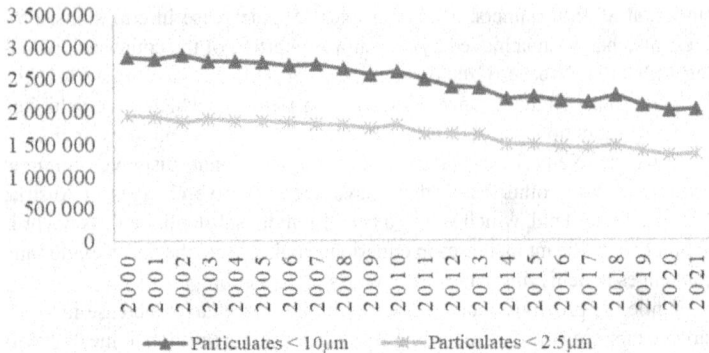

Figure 3.2 PM$_{10}$ and PM$_{2.5}$ trends

Source: Own study based on the data from Eurostat (2024a)

as a critical indicator for assessing the effectiveness of actions taken. Let us, therefore, take a closer look at the air pollution trends of EU countries.

The data provided represents annual PM emissions with aerodynamic diameters less than 10 micrometres (PM$_{10}$) and less than 2.5 micrometres (PM$_{2.5}$) in the EU from 2000 to 2021 (see: Figure 3.2). PM$_{10}$ and PM$_{2.5}$ are critical air quality indicators and represent significant public health and environmental protection challenges. Efforts to reduce their emissions and concentrations require comprehensive strategies that address various pollution sources and prioritize measures to protect vulnerable populations and sensitive ecosystems.

Sources of PM$_{10}$ include vehicular emissions, industrial activities, construction sites, agricultural operations, and natural sources such as dust storms and wildfires. PM$_{2.5}$ (Particulate Matter 2.5 micrometres or less) consists of fine particles that are smaller and more harmful than PM$_{10}$ due to their ability to penetrate deeper into the lungs and bloodstream. Sources of PM$_{2.5}$ are similar to those of PM$_{10}$ but also include combustion processes such as vehicle exhaust, industrial emissions, and residential heating. PM$_{2.5}$ is associated with a wide range of health problems, including respiratory and cardiovascular diseases, lung cancer, and premature death. Also, PM$_{2.5}$ contributes to visibility impairment, acid deposition, and nutrient imbalances in ecosystems, adversely affecting vegetation, water quality, and wildlife.

The analysis of PM$_{10}$ and PM$_{2.5}$ concentration trends shows a general downward trend in most countries studied, possibly due to the introduction of stricter air quality standards and emission reduction measures. However, there are differences between countries, which may be due to different regulatory strategies and varying levels of economic development and energy use. In some countries, such as Hungary, Lithuania, Romania and Poland, there was no significant downward or upward trend in PM$_{10}$ and PM$_{2.5}$ concentrations over the period analysed. This means that in these countries, the direction of change in air pollution concentrations cannot be determined from statistical analysis. The remaining countries have a minimal, even close to zero, decreasing trend (see Annexe 3.1).

Emissions of atmospheric pollutants such as NO_x, SO_x, ammonia and NMVOCs are some of the primary sources of PM_{10} and $PM_{2.5}$ formation through chemical and physical processes in the atmosphere. For example, NO_x react with ammonia in the atmosphere to form $PM_{2.5}$ particles through a process known as acid neutralization. Often, these substances come from the same or similar emission sources, such as road transport, industry, energy, agriculture, and natural processes (e.g., volcanic eruptions). Internal combustion vehicles and industry are the primary sources of NO_x and PM emissions. Both PM_{10} and $PM_{2.5}$, as well as chemical compounds such as NO_x, SO_x, ammonia and NMVOCs, can hurt human health, causing respiratory and cardiovascular diseases, as well as increasing the risk of cancer. In addition, these substances can also harm the environment, leading to soil acidification, water pollution, climate change, and ecosystem degradation.

Nitrogen oxides (NO^x) are a group of nitric oxide (NO) and nitrogen dioxide (NO_2), primarily emitted from combustion processes in vehicles, industrial facilities, and power plants. NO_x emissions contribute to the formation of ground-level ozone and PM, which have adverse effects on human health and the environment. Sulphur oxides (SO_x) primarily consist of sulphur dioxide (SO_2) and are emitted from various sources, including the combustion of fossil fuels (mainly coal and oil) in power plants and industrial processes. Methane VOCs include a variety of organic compounds that can contribute to the formation of ground-level ozone and secondary organic aerosols, which have implications for air quality and human health (Eurostat, 2024a).

From 2000 to 2021, there has been a general decreasing trend in the emissions mentioned above in the EU. Emissions have declined steadily over the years, indicating efforts to reduce pollution and improve regional air quality. The magnitude of reduction varies over time, with more significant declines observed in the earlier years (e.g., 2000–2010) compared to more recent years (e.g., 2010–2021). This suggests that while initial measures have been more effective in reducing emissions, further progress has been slower and more challenging.

Ammonia is a compound composed of nitrogen and hydrogen, primarily emitted from agricultural activities such as livestock farming, fertilizer application, and manure management. On the other hand, from 2000 to 2021, there was a generally stable trend in ammonia emissions in the EU, with fluctuations observed over time but no apparent overall increase or decrease. This suggests that efforts to control and reduce ammonia emissions have been less pronounced than other air pollutants such as SO_x and NO_x.

In order to acknowledge that the EU is on track to meet its emissions targets, one cannot stop at the measures implemented. After all, in the light of the

Green Deal, its goal is climate neutrality, which it wants to achieve by 2030. The EU's goal for CO_2 emissions in the Green Deal was to reduce emissions by at least 55% by 2030 compared to 1990 levels. This target was updated in 2023 from the original assumption of 40%. It is achieving net climate neutrality by 2050, which means that CO_2 emissions will not exceed the natural absorption capacity of forests and other ecosystems.

Although it is too early to determine definitively which countries within the EU will have achieved the 55% emission reduction target for 2030 (European Parliament, 2021), some countries like Estonia and Denmark were making significant progress and are close to achieving the total 55% reduction. It is important to note that reaching the 55% target requires ongoing efforts from all member states. While achieving it by 2030 is the ultimate aim, individual countries may progress at different paces due to factors like starting points, economic structures, and implemented policies.

Also, judging whether EU countries will achieve air pollution goals is difficult. The EU has established a very ambitious plan of zero pollution by 2050 (European Commission. Directorate General for Environment. et al., 2021) for air, water and soil pollution to be reduced to levels which will no longer be considered as harmful to health and natural ecosystems.

3.2 Factors to reduce air pollution in the EU countries

Analysis of CO_2 emission and air pollution trends in the EU member states have shown a need to continue efforts to protect the climate. Diagnosing factors that have determined the necessary changes in the policies of member states is crucial in the fight against ramping up the planet's temperature and improving air quality. In the available literature, authors highlight the importance of many factors influencing CO_2 emissions and air pollution. One can say that factors can be broadly categorized into three main areas: energy consumption, economic activity, and land-use changes.

The factors identified for the destruction of the environment by industrial usage are linked to energy – and, therefore, should be considered also from an economic perspective. Burning fossil fuels emits large amounts of GHG such as CO_2, CH_4 and N_2O, contributing to global warming and climate change (Tomala, 2023, p. 45). They can also cause air (Kampa & Castanas, 2008, pp. 362–367) and water pollution (Pandey, 2006, pp. 128–134). Also, it releases toxic gases such as CO, SO^2 and nitrous oxide N_2O, which can harm human health and the environment. In addition, the exploration and production of fossil fuels can contaminate groundwater and soil (Bojar et al., 2023). The above-mentioned reasons have influenced the EU's decision that RES have the potential to provide a reliable and clean energy supply.

Transitioning away from fossil fuels and reducing emissions leads to improved air quality. This has significant health benefits, as the EU's primary public health concern is poor air quality. It should be noted that the effects of air pollution depend on the type and level of pollutants and the duration of exposure. Prolonged exposure to polluted air can lead to respiratory problems, including shortness of breath, cough, bronchitis, asthma (Pawankar, 2014, pp. 1–3), and many other diseases, such as an increased risk of respiratory infections and a higher risk of cancer (Bernstein et al., 2004, pp. 1116–1123). Furthermore, it affects children and pregnant women, particularly vulnerable to pollution (Neidell, 2004, pp. 1209–1236).

As early as the 18th century, Malthus noted the connection between population growth and natural resources. According to the Malthusian theory, the food supply would not rise as much as population growth so that they may run out (Welling, 1888, pp. 1–24). On this basis, it can be pointed out that agriculture, especially livestock production, contributes to GHG emissions. This is due to deforestation, CH_4 emissions from livestock and N_2O emissions from fertilizers due to population growth and increasing food demand (Doğan, 2019, pp. 257–271; Lin & Xu, 2018, pp. 15–27; Waheed et al., 2018, pp. 4231–4238). Malthus' theory was used in the 20th century by Paul Ehrlich. According to Ehrlich, the environment, not the food supply, should play a vital role in the population (Ehrlich, 1968, pp. 3–17). Ehrlich suggested that the human population was rapidly moving towards total environmental collapse because privileged people were consuming or polluting various environmental resources, such as water and air. According to Griffiths, some theories are less focused on the pessimistic hypothesis that the world's population will meet a detrimental challenge to sustaining itself (Griffiths et al., 2012, pp. 1245–1253). An example is the Cornucopian theory, which scoffs at the idea of humans wiping themselves out; it asserts that human ingenuity can resolve any environmental or social issues that develop. Scientists can determine how to improve plant growth (Simon, 1996, pp. 564–565).

Marquette emphasises conceptual thinking on population and the environment in both social and natural sciences has traditionally been constrained by the long-standing opposition between 'Malthusian' and 'Cornucopian' perspectives (Marquette, 1997, p. 1). After publishing the Brundtland Report in 1987 (World Commission on Environment and Development, 1987), the issues of population, development, and environment have increasingly evolved in public and scientific debates. Contrary to the Malthusian approach, the Boserupian theory explains that high population density is a prerequisite for technological innovations in agriculture, leading to better agricultural production allocation. Trying to explain the transition between these two different regimes, Kögel and Prskawetz underline the role of industrialization, which allowed the escape of the Malthusian regime (Kögel & Prskawetz, 2001, p. 337). It should be noted that developments in technology can have a significant impact on emissions issues. Scientific development at the beginning of the 21st century was abundant in inventions related to the possibility of producing energy from renewable sources such as photovoltaic panels, heat pumps, and biogas plants, which can effectively replace traditional heat sources such as coal, oil, or natural gas. More importantly, technological possibilities for zero-emission energy production are now being used in many spheres of human activity. There is a growing chance that they can have an impact on emissions from production, transport, and thermal energy issues and deforestation caused by the use of wood for fuel and forest fires due to a warming climate (Birdsall, 1992, pp. 1–19; Murthy et al., 1997, pp. 327–354).

The theoretical concepts above confirm the importance of land-use changes in influencing CO_2 emissions and air pollution. However, these are not the only factors that determine ecological changes. The available literature also points to the importance of economic activity in the ecological dimension. Many studies address this issue from different perspectives, which implies diverse conclusions.

Traditional conceptions of development indicated a strong correlation between economic growth and CO_2 emissions. Researchers explained that energy consumption (often based on fossil fuels) increased with economic growth, leading to higher emissions. Appiah et al., for instance, investigated the causal link between energy use and carbon emissions for selected emerging economies from 1971–2013. They noted that non-renewable energy increased the carbon stock, but using renewable energy and industrialization improved ecology (Appiah et al., 2019, pp. 7896–7912). Similar correlations also exist between low- and middle-income countries, as confirmed by studies of Malaysia (Ang, 2008, pp. 271–278) and Turkey (Gokmenoglu & Sadeghieh, 2019, pp. 7–28).

According to Neumayer (Neumayer, 2001, pp. 147–177), the share of industries in the economy leads to environmental pollution because this sector creates higher pollution than services. In turn, Lamla inferred that the more labour-intensive the industry, the more breaches of environmental regulations would occur, leading to higher pollution (Lamla, 2009, pp. 135–144). This fascinating argument indicates that many profit-oriented companies could avoid environmental and human health responsibility. At present, this factor may be difficult to verify. However, it can be assumed that the situation will change in the next few years thanks to the implementation of the concept of corporate social responsibility in the EU (Tomala, 2022, pp. 579–586). The development of technologies enabling sustainable energy production has contributed to the debate on the energy mix of countries. Therefore, Kim and Kim discussed the impacts of energy mix, industrial structure, and production technology (Kim & Kim, 2012, pp. 1724–1741). Furthermore, they developed a PCII index (Potential Carbon Intensity Improvement) to estimate the potential of CO_2 emission reductions.

Alongside the analysed energy consumption and production and land use changes, economic growth is one of the most significant variables in environmental issues. In 1995, Grossman and Krueger used the Environmental Kuznets Curve (EKC) to assess the relationship between economic activities and environmental pollution. They proved that higher growth is accompanied by higher pollution in the early stages of economic development, but over time, the implementation of technologies helps improve air quality (Grossman & Krueger, 1995, pp. 353–377). The theory put forward by Krueger and Grossman has encouraged researchers worldwide to verify the hypothesis posed therein using examples from selected countries. Interestingly, the research results obtained by the scholars are contradictory and depend on the economic growth level (Przychodzen & Przychodzen, 2020). According to Sulich and Sołoducho-Pelc, there are organizations that implement sustainable strategies towards sustainable development (SD) despite their main activities, which are the energy sector (Sulich & Sołoducho-Pelc, 2021, pp. 1–21). Green investments rely heavily on the renewable energy sector, which, along with traditional energy sources, forms the foundation of a robust domestic economy. Technological advancements for harnessing biomass, wind, solar, and hydropower have been happening globally. By embracing renewable energy sources (RES) to combat climate change, countries can achieve SD and unlock economic benefits, both directly and indirectly (Szlávik et al., 2005, pp. 93–105).

Another critical factor analysed in the literature is the issue of transport, which plays a critical role in renewable energy usage. Currently, transport relies heavily on fossil fuels and accounts for around one-fifth of global CO_2 emissions (24% if we only consider CO_2 emissions from energy) (Ritchie, 2020). The IEA reports that 2018 renewables only accounted for 3.4% of the transport sector's energy demand. Cars and trucks are the biggest polluters on the road, making up 75% of transport emissions. Cars and buses are the worst offenders, responsible for nearly half (45.1%) of these emissions, while trucks contribute 29.4%. Even though aeroplanes are a frequent topic when discussing climate change, they contribute a smaller share (only 11.6%) of transport emissions, releasing roughly 1 billion tonnes of CO_2 annually (around 2.5% of global emissions). Ships are similar at 10.6%. On the other hand, trains and freight on rails are much cleaner, producing only 1% of transport emissions. Other transportation methods, primarily pipelines for materials like water, oil, and gas, account for a minor 2.2% (International Energy Agency, 2019). Therefore, electric vehicles (EVs) are a promising solution powered by renewable electricity. While there is still a tiny fraction of vehicles on the road, their adoption is rapidly increasing. More renewable energy sources like solar and wind power can create cleaner electricity to power EVs and potentially even electric trains and aeroplanes in the future. Also, building charging stations for EVs and adapting grids to handle RES is crucial for broader adoption. Overall, transport is a key area for increasing renewable energy usage. We can move towards a cleaner transportation sector by addressing challenges and developing solutions like EVs and a robust renewable energy infrastructure.

Based on the analysis, it is worthy analysing factors which are responsible for environmental problems in the EU. Due to data availability, the study uses Eurostat data for EU member states (27) from 2014 to 2021. The Eurostat database publishes data on climate change, such as GHG emissions, drivers, mitigation, impact and adaptation, and climate action initiatives. There are 79 variables in the database, but a preliminary screening based on data availability and including country categories allowed the selection of 24 indicators for the survey. An analysis of the factors will assess the impact of climate change on EU countries. It will, thus, make it possible to identify and implement effective strategies to reduce GHG emissions. Indeed, exploratory factor analysis (EFA) aims to reduce the 24 variables used in the study to a smaller number of unobserved characteristics (variables), which we will call factors.

The first step in the study is to check the feasibility of the analysis. A tool that helps assess whether the data is suitable for EFA is the Kaiser-Meyer-Olkin (KMO) test. EFA is a statistical technique used to identify underlying factors that explain the relationships between multiple observed variables related to climate change. KMO helps determine if the data has enough common variance among these variables for EFA to be effective and should be higher than 0.5. The results of the test are shown in Table 3.2.

Summarizing the analysis results, 16 factors were qualified for the next stage, meeting the assumptions (> 0.5). It is worth noting that the Measures for Sampling Adequacy (MSA) is 0.79 and meets the requirements of the study (0.7). Another test to carry out factor analysis is Bartlett's test. The null hypothesis in the test states that all correlations in the test are not statistically significant (equal to 0). The result of the analysis is p-value =0, which means that the test is statistically significant. Uniquenesses were then diagnosed through factor analysis, which helped identify factors to be eliminated. The survey used the following factors:

- net GHG emissions;
- air emissions intensities;
- new zero-emission vehicles by type of vehicle and type of motor energy;
- share of energy from renewable sources;
- liquid biofuels production capacities;
- solar thermal collectors' surface;
- heat pumps – technical characteristics by technologies;
- climate-related economic losses by type of event.

Once the assumptions have been met, the study can proceed to the next stage, where several factors should be considered. Eigenvalues are numerical values associated with factors in EFA. They represent the amount of variance explained by that particular component/factor. In this case, the first eigenvalue (3.0437618) is the highest, indicating that the first component/factor explains the most variance in the data. The eigenvalues generally decrease in magnitude, signifying that subsequent components/factors explain progressively less variance. The second eigenvalue (1.5107159) suggests that this two-underlying dimension can capture a substantial portion of the variation in the data. A common rule of thumb is to retain components/factors that explain

Table 3.2 Result of exploratory factor analysis

No	Factors	KMO	Uniquenesses
1	Net greenhouse gas emissions	0.51	0.634
2	Air emissions accounts	0.79	0.008
3	Air emissions account totals bridging to emission inventory totals	0.50	–
4	Air emissions intensities	0.67	0.745
5	Greenhouse gas emissions from agriculture	0.18	–
6	Primary energy consumption	0.84	0.005
7	Final energy consumption	0.8	0.005
8	Final energy consumption in transport by type of fuel	0.87	0.005
9	Complete energy balances	0.83	0.005
10	Share of fossil fuels in gross available energy	0.44	–
11	Share of fuels in final energy consumption	0.29	–
12	Production of electricity and derived heat by type of fuel	0.79	0.005
13	Electricity production capacities by main fuel groups and operator	0.81	0.005
14	Critical indicators of physical energy flow accounts	0.89	0.061
15	New zero-emission vehicles by type of vehicle and type of motor energy	0.73	0.424
16	Share of new zero-emission vehicles in all new vehicles of the same type, by type of vehicle and type of motor energy	0.49	–
17	Bovine population	0.81	0.08
18	Share of energy from renewable sources	0.66	0.288
19	Electricity production capacities for renewables and wastes	0.77	0.054
20	Liquid biofuel production capacities	0.8	0.141
21	Solar thermal collectors' surface	0.91	0.107
22	Heat pumps – technical characteristics by technologies	0.92	0.376
23	Environmental taxes by economic activity	0.93	0.005
24	Climate-related economic losses by type of event	0.86	0.451

Source: Own study

a cumulative total of, for example, about 70% of the variance. Therefore, the following eigenvalues, such as third and fourth from all (third – 0.8638451, fourth – fifth – 0.6961996, sixth – 0.4641821, seventh – 0.2524703, and eight – 0.1955197), could be considered that allow to explain a cumulative total of, for example, about 70% of the variance. The scree plot is presented in Figure 3.3. This is a visual representation of the eigenvalues.

Non Graphical Solutions to Scree Test

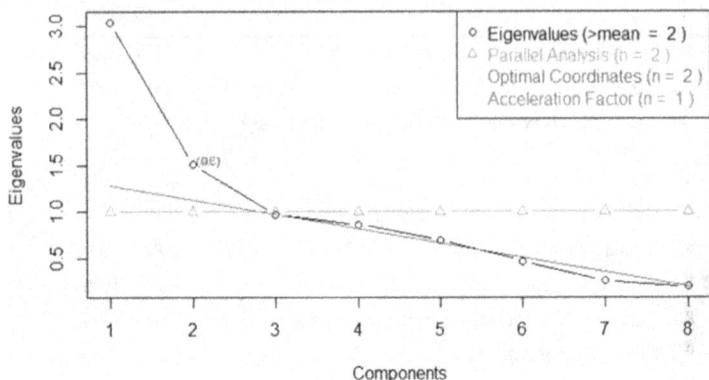

Figure 3.3 Visual representation of the eigenvalues
Source: Own study

Table 3.3 The result of factor analysis

Factor Analysis	Factor 1	Factor 2	Factor 3	Factor 4
SS loadings	1.566	1.331	1.267	0.898
Proportion Var	0.196	0.166	0.158	0.112
Cumulative Var	0.196	0.362	0.520	0.633

Source: Own study

The x-axis represents the number of components or factors extracted from the data. The y-axis represents the eigenvalues and numerical values associated with each component/factor. They represent the amount of variance explained by that particular component/factor. In a scree plot, an "elbow" shows where the eigenvalues start to level off or decrease much more slowly. The number of components/factors to retain is usually before the elbow. This is because the components/factors after the elbow explain much less variance and are likely not very informative. In the study, the two or three components explain the most variance, followed by a significant drop in the fourth component. This suggests that tree components might capture a significant portion of the variation in the data, and it might be considered to retain only those components for further analysis. The results of the factor analysis are presented in Table 3.3.

The eigenvalue criterion, the so-called Kaiser criterion, indicates that it should be included two factors in the model. However, the mentioned two factors allow us to explain only 36% of the variance. Three factors allow for 52% of the variance, while four allow for 63%. In this case, test the hypothesis that

Table 3.4 Loadings

Loadings:	Factor 1	Factor 2	Factor 3	Factor 4
Net greenhous e gas emissions			−0.507	−0.228
Air emissions intensities	−0.113	−0.148	−0.107	−0.234
New zero-emission vehicles by type of vehicle and type of motor energy	0.739	0.258		0.182
Share of energy from renewable sources		0.696	0.989	−0.130
Liquid biofuel production capacities	0.207		−0.112	0.534
Solar thermal collectors' surface	0.431	0.835		
Heat pumps – technical characteristics by technologies	0.175			0.626
Climate-related economic losses by type of event	0.865	0.226		0.243

Source: Own study

four factors are sufficient. The chi-square statistic is 6.21 on 2 degrees of freedom. The p-value is 0.0448. The loadings for each factor are shown below.

Loadings indicate how strongly a variable is associated with a particular factor (see: Table 3.4). Here is a breakdown of the loadings for the following factors. Based on the loadings, Factor 1 appears to represent a dimension related to Climate Change Mitigation Efforts:

- high positive loadings:
- new zero-emission vehicles (0.739): this solid favourable loading suggests a clear association with Factor 1. Higher adoption of new zero-emission vehicles contributes to this factor;
- climate-related economic losses (0.865): this highly favourable loading might seem counterintuitive. However, positive loadings can also indicate a shared underlying cause in EFA. In this case, it might suggest that regions with higher climate-related economic losses are also likely to make mitigation efforts (e.g., investing in new zero-emission vehicles) to address climate change. In the context of ranking, this variable was treated as unfavourable because we want to rate regions with lower climate-related economic losses as better, i.e., positive for the category "effectiveness in reducing climate-related economic losses";
- other variables: loadings for share of energy from renewable sources (positive), liquid biofuels production capacities (positive), and solar thermal collectors' surface (positive) are also positive, suggesting they contribute to Factor 1 to some extent, albeit not as strongly as new zero-emission vehicles;
- negative loadings (weaker association):
- air emissions intensities: the negative loading here is relatively weak (−0.113) and might not be very informative for interpreting Factor 1.

Factor 1 captures a dimension where higher loadings indicate a stronger association with climate change mitigation efforts. This includes focusing on new zero-emission vehicles, RES, and potentially other mitigation strategies (reflected in economic losses). Based on the loadings for Factor 2, it appears to represent a dimension related to "Renewable Energy Infrastructure":

- high positive loadings:
- solar thermal collectors' surface (0.835): this solid favourable loading suggests a clear association with Factor 2. Higher use of solar thermal collectors contributes to this factor;
- liquid biofuel production capacities (0.696): this highly favourable loading indicates that regions/countries with higher capacities for liquid biofuel production score high on Factor 2;
- moderate positive loadings:
- share of energy from renewable sources (positive): this suggests some association with RES, but not as strong as the previous two variables;
- weaker associations:
- new zero-emission vehicles (0.258): the favourable loading here is weaker than Factor 1, suggesting a less prominent role in Factor 2;
- air emissions intensities, heat pumps, climate-related economic losses: The loadings for these variables are close to zero and might not be very informative for interpreting Factor 2.

Factor 2 captures a dimension where higher loadings indicate a stronger focus on building renewable energy infrastructure. This includes focusing on solar thermal collectors, liquid biofuel production, and potentially other RES (reflected in the share of renewable energy). The loadings for Factor 3 suggest a dimension related to "Focus on Reducing Emissions through Renewables":

- dominant positive loading:
- share of energy from renewable sources (0.989): this highly favourable loading is the strongest in your provided set. It suggests a strong association between a higher share of renewable energy and Factor 3;
- negative loadings:
- net GHG emissions (-0.507): this negative loading indicates that higher values on Factor 3 are associated with lower net GHG emissions. This aligns with the idea that using more RES can reduce emissions.
- air emissions intensities (-0.107): the negative loading here is weaker and might not be very informative for interpreting Factor 3;

- loadings close to zero:
- the remaining variables (liquid biofuels, solar thermal collectors, heat pumps, climate losses) have loadings close to zero, suggesting they are not strongly associated with Factor 3.

Factor 3 captures a dimension where a higher share of energy from renewable sources is the key driver. This suggests that regions/countries focusing more on RES score high on Factor 3. Consequently, these regions/countries might also have lower net GHG emissions (negative loading).

Based on the provided loadings for Factor 4, interpreting its meaning is more challenging than the previous factors. There are two possible interpretations for Factor 4, depending on the emphasis you place on the loadings:

- focus on biofuels and heat technologies: this interpretation highlights:
- positive loadings: liquid biofuels production capacities (0.534), heat pumps (0.626). These positive loadings suggest an association with Factor 4. Regions/countries focusing more on biofuel production and heat pump technologies might score higher on this factor.
- weak and uncertain dimension:
- loadings close to zero: Most loadings are relatively close to zero, including: Net GHG emissions (-0.228), air emissions intensities (-0.234), Share of renewable energy (-0.130). This suggests these variables are not strongly associated with Factor 4.

Summarizing the above, it can be noted that four factors appear to capture different aspects of climate change mitigation efforts and their potential outcomes. Factor 1 (Climate et al.) emphasises new zero-emission vehicles and potentially other mitigation strategies (reflected in economic losses). Higher loadings indicate a stronger association with efforts to address climate change. Factor 2 (Renewable Energy Infrastructure) focuses on building infrastructure for RES, particularly solar thermal collectors and liquid biofuels. Higher loadings indicate a stronger focus on this type of infrastructure. The share of energy from renewable sources heavily drives Factor 3 (Focus on Reducing Emissions through Renewables). Regions/ countries focusing more on renewables score high on this factor, potentially leading to lower net GHG emissions (negative loading). Factor 4 (Uncertain Interpretation) meaning is less clear. It might capture a focus on biofuels and heat pump technologies, but the loadings are weaker compared to other factors.

Also, it should be noted that there might be some overlap between the factors. For example, Factor 1 (mitigation efforts) and Factor 2 (renewable infrastructure) could be related, as new zero-emission vehicles might require a supporting infrastructure for clean energy. Factor 3 (renewables and emissions) seems distinct, focusing solely on the share of renewable energy and its potential impact on emissions. Factor 4's relationship with other factors is unclear and requires further exploration.

It is worth examining the countries in terms of their efficiency and their commitment to EU objectives. Who are the EU's leaders, marauders, or averages in green transformation?

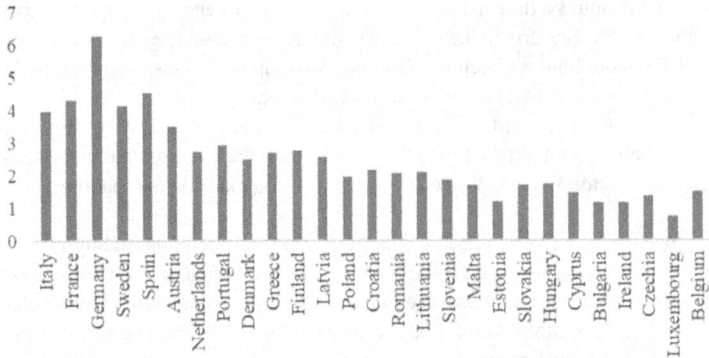

Figure 3.4 Average of Green Deal Factor between 2014 and 2021

Source: Own study

Based on factor analysis, a ranking of countries for 2021 was established, considering the aggregated four factors, counting the sum on a scale between 0 and 10 (see Annexe 3.1). The Figure 3.4 shows the average analysis results for the "Green Deal Factor" during 2014 and 2021.

In Figure 3.4 one can see a country's average towards environmentally friendly policies, sustainability initiatives, or adherence to green energy goals. Germany is at the forefront of the green shift and achieves a much higher average than other EU countries. Countries with higher Green Deal Factors, such as France (4.31), Spain (4.51), Sweden (4.13), Italy (3.97) and Austria (3.51), have demonstrated more robust dedication to implementing green policies and transitioning towards sustainable practices during 2014–2021. We can call them leaders of the green transformation. They show significant efforts towards green initiatives, although not as high as Germany.

Countries with lower Green Deal Factors (between 2.0 and 3.0), such as Portugal (2.92), Finland (2.75), Netherlands (2.72), Greece (2.69), Latvia (2.56), Denmark (2.5), Lithuania (2.08), Romania (2.05) have had less emphasis on green policies or faced challenges in implementing them effectively.

Some countries, like Poland (1.95), Slovenia (1.85), Hungary (1.72), Malta (1.71), Slovakia (1.68), Belgium (1.48), Czechia (1.36), Estonia (1.19), Cyprus (1.46), Bulgaria (1.17), and Ireland (1.17) appear to have relatively low Green Deal Factors, suggesting potential areas for improvement in their sustainability agendas. Luxembourg (0.73) has a relatively low level of commitment or progress towards environmental sustainability compared to other European countries. This indicates that Luxembourg has been less proactive or effective in implementing policies and initiatives aimed at addressing environmental issues and promoting sustainability.

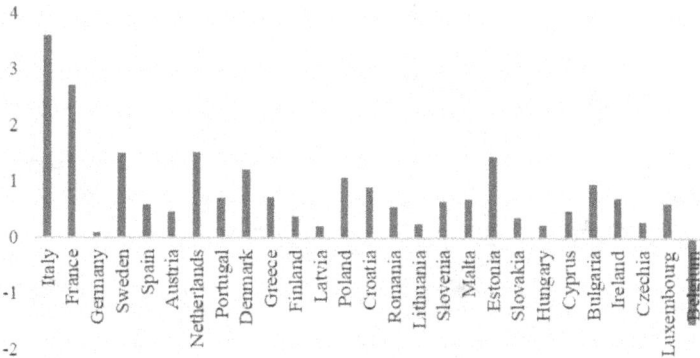

Figure 3.5 EU countries progress towards environmental sustainability
Source: Own study

Overall, the data reflects varying levels of commitment among European countries towards environmental sustainability and green initiatives. It is also worth considering which countries have made the most progress and whose efforts have been negligible. The Figure 3.5 shows the results of the analysis in this respect.

Figure 3.5 indicates the change in a country's commitment or progress towards environmental sustainability and addressing climate change between 2014 and 2021. Positive values indicate an increase in commitment or progress, while negative values indicate a decrease. The data suggests that most listed countries have increased their commitment or progress towards environmental sustainability and addressing climate change between 2014 and 2021, with varying degrees of change. However, the 2021 indicator for Belgium differs significantly from its performance in the other years studied. Although Germany achieved the highest Green Deal Factor, it was not among the leaders who made the most significant progress during the period under review. Italy and France achieved the best results in this aspect. In contrast, the most minor progress is seen in Germany, Hungary, the Czech Republic, Lithuania, and Latvia.

3.3 Impact of COVID-19 and Russian invasion of Ukraine

The achievement of the climate targets that the EU set itself back in 2009 has not occurred under stable and undisturbed conditions. As Taleb points out, in order to understand a phenomenon, it is first necessary to look at extreme situations, especially when, as in the case of the Black Swans, their cumulative impact on the environment can be enormous (Taleb & Taleb 2016, p. 27).

The two crises of COVID-19 and the war in Ukraine have significantly impacted climate change in various ways. This was corroborated by Prokop, who indicated that the global spread of the COVID-19 epidemic and its escalation to a pandemic undoubtedly posed a significant challenge for European countries in protecting the lives and health of their citizens while striving to prevent the destabilization of state economies due to the implemented restrictions (Tomala et al., 2022, p. 1). Each country of the EU member state acted on the new situation, which had to guarantee political, social, and economic stability. Although the COVID-19 crisis was not over, countries faced another unpredictable situation: the outbreak of war in Ukraine. The World Bank's report states that the war in Ukraine has led to a massive humanitarian crisis, with over 12 million people displaced and more than 13 million in urgent need of humanitarian aid. Ukraine's economy is in ruins, and the population's trauma will have long-lasting effects (Guenette et al., 2022, p. 3).

The COVID-19 pandemic understandably diverted attention from climate change mitigation efforts as governments and societies focused on immediate health and economic concerns. Similarly, the conflict in Ukraine unfocussed attention from global climate change discussions and cooperation, as countries became preoccupied with geopolitical tensions and security issues, connecting with energy dependency. Also, both crises have highlighted the interconnectedness of global challenges and the need for resilient and sustainable solutions. The pandemic underscored the importance of investing in healthcare systems, social safety nets, and resilient infrastructure, which are also critical for climate adaptation and mitigation. Additionally, geopolitical tensions arising from the conflict in Ukraine influenced international climate negotiations and cooperation, impacting the implementation of global climate policies and agreements. The conflict has caused widespread repercussions worldwide, affecting various sectors such as commodity markets, trade, financial transactions, displaced populations, and market sentiment. Nearby regions faced significant challenges due to a surge in refugees, straining essential services.

It is, therefore, worth taking a closer look at how the two "Black Swans" have influenced the key factors determining the success of Green Deal policies. Firstly, both crises have led to a reduction in economic activity globally. Lockdowns and restrictions imposed to curb the spread of COVID-19 resulted in decreased industrial production, transportation, and energy consumption (Mofijur et al., 2021, pp. 343–359; Nundy et al., 2021, pp. 1–24). Similarly, the conflict in Ukraine disrupted trade and economic stability in the region (Basuki, 2023, pp. 277–299; Singh, 2022, pp. 1–15). The Table 3.5 presents data on the issue of energy consumption, industrial production and energy use in transport.

The Table 3.5 shows fluctuations in energy consumption over the years. There was an overall increasing trend from 2011 to 2019, followed by a notable decrease in 2020, likely influenced by factors such as changes in transportation patterns, economic conditions, and policy interventions connected with COVID-19. Then, a recovery or rebound was observed in 2021 and

Table 3.5 Trends of energy consumption and production in industry

	Production in industry	Final energy consumption in transport by type of fuel	Final energy consumption
2011		278 859.112	985.2
2012		269 085.076	983.2
2013		265 347.632	981.0
2014	97.4	268 718.554	939.2
2015	100.0	272 408.520	958.6
2016	101.8	278 670.070	977.6
2017	105.1	284 540.635	989.8
2018	106.4	285 948.525	992.5
2019	106.2	288 654.895	986.5
2020	98.5	251 380.184	906.3
2021	107.5	272 022.360	967.4
2022	110.8	279 567.080	940.5

Source: Own study based on Eurostat (2022c, 2022b, 2024b)

2022, but not enough to achieve the level from 2019. Similar trends but not as strong as observed for final energy consumption and production in industry. Researchers underline that reducing economic activity translates to emissions of GHG and pollutants, thereby temporarily mitigating climate change (Imran et al., 2023, pp. 01–07; Pereira et al., 2022, p. 155865; Rawtani et al., 2022, p. 157932; Samaras et al., 2019, p. 100409).

Secondly, the COVID-19 pandemic led to a temporary decline in the demand for fossil fuels such as oil and coal as industries slowed down and transportation activities decreased (Le Billon et al., 2021, pp. 1347–1356; Smith et al., 2021, p. 105170). However, there were fluctuations in renewable energy investments and consumption patterns. The war in Ukraine further exacerbated energy concerns, particularly in Europe, leading to discussions on diversifying energy sources and reducing reliance on fossil fuels (Ateed, 2024, pp. 119–138). Management within the renewable energy sector in the European Union (EU) encompasses a multifaceted interaction involving policies, regulations, technological advancements, and market dynamics. The EU has led efforts to promote RES to combat climate change and reduce reliance on fossil fuels. The share of renewable energy consumption has steadily increased over the past decade. It started at 16% in 2013 and reached 23% in 2022. There appears to be a slight increase in the share of renewable energy consumption between 2019 and 2020, which means that COVID-19 positively influenced the result (Eurostat, 2022d).

Existing literature on management within the EU's renewable energy sector offers insights into its current status, challenges, and future trajectories – a critical component of the EU's energy policy (da Graça Carvalho,

2012, pp. 19–22). Recent studies underscore the significance of EU-wide renewable energy targets, particularly the shift from the earlier 20–20–20 targets to the more ambitious 2030 objectives (Ćetković & Buzogány, 2016, pp. 642–657). Scholars frequently stress the importance of establishing clear, stable, and coherent policy frameworks to attract investments into the sector (Tomala, 2024, pp. 551–570). Conversely, there is discussion among researchers regarding the diverse approaches of member states in achieving renewable energy targets (Haas, 2019, pp. 200–210). Some nations excel in specific technologies, such as Denmark in wind power (Mey & Diesendorf, 2018, pp. 108–117), Italy in geothermal energy (Manzella et al., 2018, pp. 232–248), and Greece in solar sources (Bellos & Tzivanidis, 2020, p. 122855), while others, like Poland (Bórawski et al., 2023, p. 726) and Hungary (Antal, 2019, pp. 162–182), lag. This kind of specialization of countries producing renewable energy can be considered forward-looking due to independence from outside countries such as Russia.

EU has a relatively high dependency on energy imports. In 2022, the EU relied on imports for 62.5% of its energy consumption. This means they produced or stockpiled only 37.5% of their energy needs. Although the level of energy import dependency by-product decreased between 2020–2021 because of the pandemic, in 2022, one can observe the opposite situation. There are several reasons for the EU's high import reliance, such as limited resources, growing demand or policy shifts. For instance, the EU lacks sufficient domestic reserves of fossil fuels like oil and natural gas. Also, energy consumption continues to rise in the EU, driven by population growth and economic activity. No less important is the policy that the EU countries made actively pursuing RES (Eurostat, 2022a).

While both crises have had short-term implications for climate change, their long-term effects will depend on how societies and governments respond, adapt, and priorities climate action in the aftermath of these challenges. It is essential to acknowledge that the ongoing conflict in Ukraine has significantly impacted the EU across various fronts, including security, economy, and societal dynamics. This conflict has fundamentally altered the EU, emerging as a more militarized, interconnected, and security-focused entity. While the long-term repercussions are yet to materialize fully, the region is undoubtedly experiencing a period of substantial transformation and uncertainty. It is crucial to recognize that the situation is dynamic, and the outlined changes are just some notable ones observed thus far. As the conflict persists, the EU's complete transformation will likely unfold over the coming years. There are more substantial and weaker members within the EU, and concerted efforts have been made to address disparities and mitigate instability, especially in Northeastern Europe. In this context, symbolic gestures, tangible actions, and cooperative endeavours among EU countries toward shared environmental goals are paramount.

Reference list

Abbasi, A., Sajid, A., Haq, N., Rahman, S., Misbah, Z., Sanober, G., Ashraf, M., & Kazi, A. G. (2014). Agricultural pollution: An emerging issue. In *Improvement of crops in the era of climatic changes: Volume 1* (pp. 347–387). Springer.

Ang, J. B. (2008). Economic development, pollutant emissions and energy consumption in Malaysia. *Journal of Policy Modeling, 30*(2), 271–278.

Antal, M. (2019). How the regime hampered a transition to renewable electricity in Hungary. *Environmental Innovation and Societal Transitions, 33*, 162–182.

Appiah, K., Du, J., Yeboah, M., & Appiah, R. (2019). Causal correlation between energy use and carbon emissions in selected emerging economies – Panel model approach. *Environmental Science and Pollution Research, 26*, 7896–7912.

Ateed, E. H. (2024). The impact of Russia-Ukraine war on the global energy crisis. In *Analyzing energy crises and the impact of country policies on the world* (pp. 119–138). IGI Global.

Basuki, L. W. (2023). Impact of the Russia Ukraine conflict on economic deglobalization. *Journal of Social Political Sciences, 4*(3), 277–299.

Bellos, E., & Tzivanidis, C. (2020). Solar concentrating systems and applications in Greece–A critical review. *Journal of Cleaner Production, 272*, 122855.

Bennetzen, E. H., Smith, P., & Porter, J. R. (2016). Agricultural production and greenhouse gas emissions from world regions – The major trends over 40 years. *Global Environmental Change, 37*, 43–55.

Bernstein, J. A., Alexis, N., Barnes, C., Bernstein, I. L., Nel, A., Peden, D., Diaz-Sanchez, D., Tarlo, S. M., Williams, P. B., & Bernstein, J. A. (2004). Health effects of air pollution. *Journal of Allergy and Clinical Immunology, 114*(5), 1116–1123. https://doi.org/10.1016/j.jaci.2004.08.030

Birdsall, N. (1992). *Another look at population and global warming* (Vol. 1020). World Bank Publications.

Bojar, W., Żarski, W., Kuśmierek-Tomaszewska, R., Żarski, J., Baranowski, P., Krzyszczak, J., Lamorski, K., Sławiński, C., Mattas, K., & Staboulis, C. (2023). A comprehensive approach to assess the impact of agricultural production factors on selected ecosystem services in Poland. *Resources, 12*(9), 99. https://doi.org/10.3390/resources12090099

Bórawski, P., Bełdycka-Bórawska, A., & Holden, L. (2023). Changes in the polish coal sector economic situation with the background of the European Union energy security and eco-efficiency policy. *Energies, 16*(2), 726.

Cazenave, A., & Llovel, W. (2010). Contemporary sea level rise. *Annual Review of Marine Science, 2*(1), 145–173. https://doi.org/10.1146/annurev-marine-120308-081105

Ćetković, S., & Buzogány, A. (2016). Varieties of capitalism and clean energy transitions in the European Union: When renewable energy hits different economic logics. *Climate Policy, 16*(5), 642–657.

Constantin, D.-E., Bocăneala, C., Voiculescu, M., Roşu, A., Merlaud, A., Roozendael, M. V., & Georgescu, P. L. (2020). Evolution of SO2 and NOx emissions from several large combustion plants in Europe during

2005–2015. *International Journal of Environmental Research and Public Health, 17*(10), 3630. https://doi.org/10.3390/ijerph17103630

da Graça Carvalho, M. (2012). EU energy and climate change strategy. *Energy, 40*(1), 19–22.

De Sario, M., Katsouyanni, K., & Michelozzi, P. (2013). Climate change, extreme weather events, air pollution and respiratory health in Europe. *European Respiratory Journal, 42*(3), 826–843.

Doğan, N. (2019). The impact of agriculture on CO_2 emissions in China. *Panoeconomicus, 66*(2), 257–271.

Ehrlich, P. (1968). *The population bomb*. Sierra Club/Ballantine Books.

European Commission. Directorate General for Environment., VVA., Toegepast natuurwetenschappelijk onderzoek., Tecnalia., ANOTEC., & Universitat Autònoma de Barcelona. (2021). *Assessment of potential health benefits of noise abatement measures in the EU: Phenomena project*. Publications Office. https://data.europa.eu/doi/10.2779/24566

European Environment Agency. (2023). *Air pollution – European Environment Agency* [Page]. https://www.eea.europa.eu/themes/air/intro

European Parliament. (2021). *Regulation (EU) 2021/1119 of the European Parliament and of the Council of 30 June 2021 establishing the framework for achieving climate neutrality and amending Regulations (EC) No 401/2009 and (EU) 2018/1999 ('European Climate Law')*. http://data.europa.eu/eli/reg/2021/1119/oj/eng

Eurostat. (2021). *Exposure to air pollution by particulate matter* [dataset]. https://ec.europa.eu/eurostat/databrowser/404-product?lang=en

Eurostat. (2022a). *Energy import dependency by products*. https://ec.europa.eu/eurostat/databrowser/view/sdg_07_50/default/table?lang=en&category=sdg.sdg_07

Eurostat. (2022b). *Final energy consumption in transport by type of fuel*. https://ec.europa.eu/eurostat/databrowser/view/ten00126/default/table?lang=en&category=cli.cli_dri.cli_dri_tran

Eurostat. (2022c). *Production in industry*. https://ec.europa.eu/eurostat/databrowser/view/STS_INPR_A/default/table?lang=en

Eurostat. (2022d). *Share of renewable energy in gross final energy consumption*. https://ec.europa.eu/eurostat/databrowser/view/SDG_07_40/default/table?lang=en

Eurostat. (2023). *Air emissions intensities*. https://ec.europa.eu/eurostat/databrowser/view/env_ac_aeint_r2/default/table?lang=en

Eurostat. (2024a). *Air pollutants by source sector*. https://ec.europa.eu/eurostat/databrowser/view/env_air_emis__custom_10751128/default/table

Eurostat. (2024b). *Final energy consumption*. https://ec.europa.eu/eurostat/databrowser/view/sdg_07_11/default/table

Fan, J., Rosenfeld, D., Yang, Y., Zhao, C., Leung, L. R., & Li, Z. (2015). Substantial contribution of anthropogenic air pollution to catastrophic floods in Southwest China. *Geophysical Research Letters, 42*(14), 6066–6075.

Gokmenoglu, K. K., & Sadeghieh, M. (2019). Financial development, CO_2 emissions, fossil fuel consumption and economic growth: The case of Turkey. *Strategic Planning for Energy and the Environment, 38*(4), 7–28.

Graham, H., Harrison, A., & Lampard, P. (2022). Public perceptions of climate change and its health impacts: Taking account of people's exposure to floods and air pollution. *International Journal of Environmental Research and Public Health*, *19*(4), 2246.

Griffiths, H., Keirns, N., Strayer, E., Sadler, T., Cody-Rydzewski, S., Scaramuzzo, G., Vyain, S., Bry, J., & Jones, F. (2012). Demography and population. In *Introduction to sociology 2e*. OSCRiceUniversity. https://wtcs.pressbooks.pub/introsociology2e/chapter/demography-and-population/

Grossman, G. M., & Krueger, A. B. (1995). Economic growth and the environment. *The Quarterly Journal of Economics*, *110*(2), 353–377.

Guenette, Justin Damien, Kenworthy, P. G., & Wheeler, C. M. (2022). *Implications of the war in Ukraine for the global economy*. World Bank. https://hdl.handle.net/10986/37372

Haas, T. (2019). Comparing energy transitions in Germany and Spain using a political economy perspective. *Environmental Innovation and Societal Transitions*, *31*, 200–210.

Imran, M., Khan, S., Jambari, H., Musah, M. B., & Zaman, K. (2023). War psychology: The global carbon emissions impact of the Ukraine-Russia conflict. *Frontiers in Environmental Science*, *11*, 1065301.

Intergovernmental Panel on Climate Change. (2023). *AR6 synthesis report: Climate change 2023*. https://www.ipcc.ch/report/ar6/syr/

International Energy Agency. (2019). *Transport sector CO_2 emissions by mode in the Sustainable Development Scenario, 2000–2030*. IEA. https://www.iea.org/data-and-statistics/charts/transport-sector-co2-emissions-by-mode-in-the-sustainable-development-scenario-2000-2030

International Energy Agency. (2022). *CO_2 emissions in 2022 – Analysis*. IEA. https://www.iea.org/reports/co2-emissions-in-2022

Johnston, F., Hanigan, I., Henderson, S., Morgan, G., & Bowman, D. (2011). Extreme air pollution events from bushfires and dust storms and their association with mortality in Sydney, Australia 1994–2007. *Environmental Research*, *111*(6), 811–816.

Kampa, M., & Castanas, E. (2008). Human health effects of air pollution. *Environmental Pollution*, *151*(2), 362–367.

Kim, K., & Kim, Y. (2012). International comparison of industrial CO_2 emission trends and the energy efficiency paradox utilizing production-based decomposition. *Energy Economics*, *34*(5), 1724–1741.

Koenigk, T., Key, J., & Vihma, T. (2020). Climate change in the Arctic. *Physics and Chemistry of the Arctic Atmosphere*, 673–705.

Kögel, T., & Prskawetz, A. (2001). Agricultural productivity growth and escape from the Malthusian trap. *Journal of Economic Growth*, *6*, 337–357.

Kubelka, V., Sandercock, B. K., Székely, T., & Freckleton, R. P. (2022). Animal migration to northern latitudes: Environmental changes and increasing threats. *Trends in Ecology & Evolution*, *37*(1), 30–41.

Lamla, M. J. (2009). Long-run determinants of pollution: A robustness analysis. *Ecological Economics*, *69*(1), 135–144.

Le Billon, P., Lujala, P., Singh, D., Culbert, V., & Kristoffersen, B. (2021). Fossil fuels, climate change, and the COVID-19 crisis: Pathways for a just and green post-pandemic recovery. *Climate Policy*, *21*(10), 1347–1356.

Letcher, T. (2021). Global warming – A complex situation. In T. Letcher (Ed.), *Climate change: Observed impacts on planet Earth.* Elsevier.

Li, W.-W. (2020). Air pollution, air quality, vehicle emissions, and environmental regulations. In *Traffic-related air pollution* (pp. 23–49). Elsevier.

Lin, B., & Xu, B. (2018). Factors affecting CO_2 emissions in China's agriculture sector: A quantile regression. *Renewable and Sustainable Energy Reviews, 94*, 15–27.

Lloyd, J., & Farquhar, G. D. (2008). Effects of rising temperatures and $[CO_2]$ on the physiology of tropical forest trees. *Philosophical Transactions of the Royal Society B: Biological Sciences, 363*(1498), 1811–1817. https://doi.org/10.1098/rstb.2007.0032

Łuszczuk, M. (2011). Climate change in the Arctic and it's geopolitical consequence-The analysis of the European Union perspective. *Papers on Global Change IGBP, 18*.

Manzella, A., Bonciani, R., Allansdottir, A., Botteghi, S., Donato, A., Giamberini, S., Lenzi, A., Paci, M., Pellizzone, A., & Scrocca, D. (2018). Environmental and social aspects of geothermal energy in Italy. *Geothermics, 72*, 232–248.

Marquette, C. (1997). *Turning but Not toppling Malthus: Boserupian theory on population and the environment relationships. Working Paper Chr. Michelsen Institute, 16*.

Mey, F., & Diesendorf, M. (2018). Who owns an energy transition? Strategic action fields and community wind energy in Denmark. *Energy Research & Social Science, 35*, 108–117.

Mofijur, M., Fattah, I. R., Alam, M. A., Islam, A. S., Ong, H. C., Rahman, S. A., Najafi, G., Ahmed, S. F., Uddin, M. A., & Mahlia, T. M. I. (2021). Impact of COVID-19 on the social, economic, environmental and energy domains: Lessons learnt from a global pandemic. *Sustainable Production and Consumption, 26*, 343–359.

Munsif, R., Zubair, M., Aziz, A., & Nadeem Zafar, M. (2021). Industrial air emission pollution: Potential sources and sustainable mitigation. In R. Viskup (Ed.), *Environmental emissions.* IntechOpen. https://doi.org/10.5772/intechopen.93104

Murthy, N., Panda, M., & Parikh, J. (1997). Economic development, poverty reduction and carbon emissions in India. *Energy Economics, 19*(3), 327–354.

Neidell, M. J. (2004). Air pollution, health, and socio-economic status: The effect of outdoor air quality on childhood asthma. *Journal of Health Economics, 23*(6), 1209–1236.

Neumayer, E. (2001). Pollution havens: An analysts of policy options for dealing with an elusive phenomenon. *The Journal of Environment & Development, 10*(2), 147–177. JSTOR. http://www.jstor.org/stable/44319542

Norby, R. J., & Luo, Y. (2004). Evaluating ecosystem responses to rising atmospheric CO_2 and global warming in a multi-factor world. *New Phytologist, 162*(2), 281–293. https://doi.org/10.1111/j.1469-8137.2004.01047.x

Nundy, S., Ghosh, A., Mesloub, A., Albaqawy, G. A., & Alnaim, M. M. (2021). Impact of COVID-19 pandemic on socio-economic, energy-environment and transport sector globally and sustainable development goal (SDG). *Journal of Cleaner Production, 312*, 127705.

Pandey, S. (2006). Water pollution and health. *Kathmandu University Medical Journal (KUMJ)*, *4*(1), 128–134.

Pawankar, R. (2014). Allergic diseases and asthma: A global public health concern and a call to action. *World Allergy Organization Journal*, *7*(1), 1–3.

Pereira, P., Bašić, F., Bogunovic, I., & Barcelo, D. (2022). Russian-Ukrainian war impacts the total environment. *Science of the Total Environment, 837*, 155865.

Przychodzen, W., & Przychodzen, J. (2020). Determinants of renewable energy production in transition economies: A panel data approach. *Energy, 191*, 116583.

Ramanathan, V. (2007). Global dimming by air pollution and global warming by greenhouse gases: Global and regional perspectives. In C. D. O'Dowd & P. E. Wagner (Eds.), *Nucleation and atmospheric aerosols* (pp. 473–483). Springer Netherlands. https://doi.org/10.1007/978-1-4020-6475-3_94

Rawtani, D., Gupta, G., Khatri, N., Rao, P. K., & Hussain, C. M. (2022). Environmental damages due to war in Ukraine: A perspective. *Science of the Total Environment, 850*, 157932.

Ritchie, H. (2020). Cars, planes, trains: Where do CO_2 emissions from transport come from? *Our World in Data*. https://ourworldindata.org/co2-emissions-from-transport

Ritchie, H., Mathieu, E., Rodés-Guirao, L., Appel, C., Giattino, C., Ortiz-Ospina, E., Hasell, J., Macdonald, B., Beltekian, D., & Roser, M. (2020). Coronavirus pandemic (COVID-19). *Our World in Data*. https://ourworldindata.org/covid-vaccinations

Sakadevan, K., & Nguyen, M.-L. (2017). Livestock production and its impact on nutrient pollution and greenhouse gas emissions. *Advances in Agronomy, 141*, 147–184.

Samaras, C., Nuttall, W. J., & Bazilian, M. (2019). Energy and the military: Convergence of security, economic, and environmental decision-making. *Energy Strategy Reviews, 26*, 100409. https://doi.org/10.1016/j.esr.2019.100409

Sathre, R. (2014). Comparing the heat of combustion of fossil fuels to the heat accumulated by their lifecycle greenhouse gases. *Fuel, 115*, 674–677. https://doi.org/10.1016/j.fuel.2013.07.069

Seebacher, F., & Post, E. (2015). Climate change impacts on animal migration. *Climate Change Responses, 2*(1), 1–2.

Simon, J. L. (1996). *The ultimate resource 2*. Princeton University Press.

Singh, S. K. (2022). Russia's Invasion of Ukraine: Disrupting Economies throughout the World. *NICE Journal of Business, 17*.

Smith, L. V., Tarui, N., & Yamagata, T. (2021). Assessing the impact of COVID-19 on global fossil fuel consumption and CO_2 emissions. *Energy Economics, 97*, 105170.

Sulich, A., & Sołoducho-Pelc, L. (2021). Renewable energy producers' strategies in the Visegrád group countries. *Energies, 14*(11), 3048. https://doi.org/10.3390/en14113048

Swapna, P., Ravichandran, M., Nidheesh, G., Jyoti, J., Sandeep, N., Deepa, J. S., & Unnikrishnan, A. S. (2020). Sea-level rise. In R. Krishnan, J. Sanjay, C. Gnanaseelan, M. Mujumdar, A. Kulkarni, & S. Chakraborty (Eds.),

Assessment of climate change over the Indian region (pp. 175–189). Springer Singapore. https://doi.org/10.1007/978-981-15-4327-2_9

Szlávik, J., Nagypál, N. C., & Pálvölgyi, T. (2005). Sustainability and business behaviour: The role of corporate social responsibility. *Periodica Polytechnica Social and Management Sciences, 13*(2), 93–105.

Taleb, N. N., & Taleb, N. N. (2016). *The black swan: The impact of the highly improbable* (Random House trade paperback ed.). Random House.

Tomala, M. (2022). Sustainable development in the strategies of polish enterprises. In: Visvizi, A., Troisi, O., Grimaldi, M. (eds) Research and Innovation Forum 2022. RIIFORUM 2022. Springer Proceedings in Complexity. Springer, Cham. https://doi.org/10.1007/978-3-031-19560-0_49 (pp. 579–586).

Tomala, M. (2023). Monitorowanie jakości powietrza w Polsce w świetle koncepcji smart city. *Środkowoeuropejskie Studia Polityczne, 1*, 45–70.

Tomala, M. (2024). Political and economic rationale for the development of renewable energy in European Union countries. *Scientific Papers of Silesian University of Technology. Organization And Management Series, 191*, 551–570. http://dx.doi.org/10.29119/1641-3466.2024.191.35

Tomala, M., Prokop, M., & Kordonska, A. (2022). *Public policy and the impact of COVID-19 in Europe: Economic, political and social dimensions* (1st ed.). Routledge.

Tsangari, H., Paschalidou, A., Kassomenos, A., Vardoulakis, S., Heaviside, C., Georgiou, K., & Yamasaki, E. (2016). Extreme weather and air pollution effects on cardiovascular and respiratory hospital admissions in Cyprus. *Science of the Total Environment, 542*, 247–253.

United Nations. (1992). *United Nations framework convention on climate change.* https://unfccc.int/files/essential_background/background_publications_htmlpdf/application/pdf/conveng.pdf

Waheed, R., Chang, D., Sarwar, S., & Chen, W. (2018). Forest, agriculture, renewable energy, and CO_2 emission. *Journal of Cleaner Production, 172*, 4231–4238.

Walsh, J. E., Overland, J. E., Groisman, P. Y., & Rudolf, B. (2011). Ongoing climate change in the Arctic. *AMBIO, 40*, 6–16.

Welling, J. C. (1888). The law of Malthus. *American Anthropologist, 1*(1), 1–24.

World Commission on Environment and Development. (1987). *Report of the World Commission on Environment and Development: Our common future.* https://www.google.com/url?sa=t&rct=j&q=&esrc=s&source=web&cd=&ved=2ahUKEwilmZaDnKD5AhVfiv0HHd5eCuQQFnoECAkQAQ&url=https%3A%2F%2Fsustainabledevelopment.un.org%2Fcontent%2Fdocuments%2F5987our-common-future.pdf&usg=AOvVaw293_rr5E8NxDhKDKPVja0e

Xu, R., Yu, P., Abramson, M. J., Johnston, F. H., Samet, J. M., Bell, M. L., Haines, A., Ebi, K. L., Li, S., & Guo, Y. (2020). Wildfires, global climate change, and human health. *New England Journal of Medicine, 383*(22), 2173–2181. https://doi.org/10.1056/NEJMsr2028985

Zhang, K., & Batterman, S. (2013). Air pollution and health risks due to vehicle traffic. *Science of the Total Environment, 450*, 307–316.

4 In-depth case studies

Magdalena Tomala

4.1 Leaders, second-raters, and marauders

While CO_2 emissions and air quality are interconnected aspects of the environment, they represent challenges with distinct implications for climate change and public health (see chapter 3). Both issues require concerted global, national, and local efforts to mitigate emissions, improve air quality, and safeguard human health and the environment. Therefore, the k-means analysis, a significant tool in this research, groups countries according to the analysing variables. A chart showing the optimal number of clusters is presented in Figure 4.1.

The Sum of Squared Errors (SSE) measures how well the clusters fit the data. A lower SSE indicates a better fit. In the ideal scenario, the number of clusters that minimise the SSE would be the number of distinct groups with similar air quality profiles within the data set. This graph shows that the optimal number of clusters is three, a finding validated by the SSE measure. After this number, the graph flattens out. This confirms the initial assumptions about the feasibility of building three clusters due to the two components. Figure 4.2 presents the division into three clusters between EU countries from 2014 to 2019.

Based on the analysis, it can be concluded that there is a high degree of convergence regarding the groups formed. It should be noted that the juxtaposition leaders are countries grouped in cluster 1. This cluster comprises Western and Northern European countries like Austria, Belgium, Denmark, Finland, France, Germany, Ireland, Italy, Luxembourg, Netherlands, Spain, and Sweden, which achieve the best results in the analysed categories. They have the lowest level of air emissions intensities and exposure to air pollution. Two Nordic countries come to the fore: Sweden and Finland. Both countries have similar pollution figures, but Sweden has twice as less CO_2 emissions as Finland. Therefore, it can be considered a leader in the Green Transition.

Homogenous groups are also formed within cluster 3. This cluster includes Croatia, Cyprus, Czechia, Greece, Hungary, Latvia, Lithuania, Portugal, Romania, Slovakia, and Slovenia. These countries have higher air emission

DOI: 10.4324/9781032707006-5

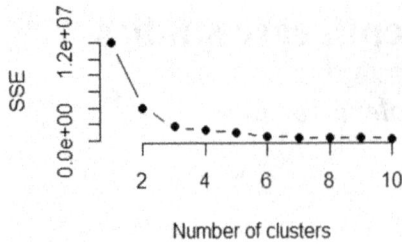

Figure 4.1 The optimal number of clusters

Source: Own study based on the data from Eurostat (2021)

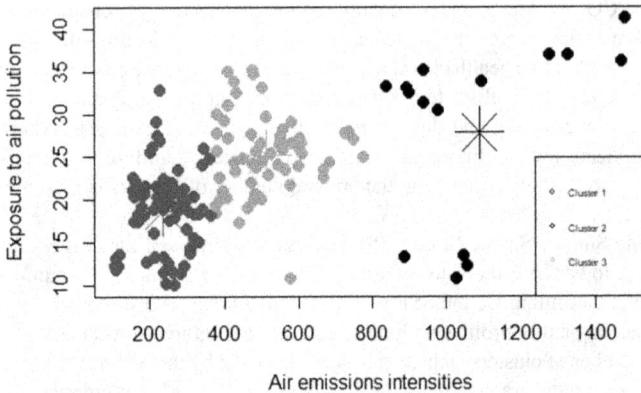

Figure 4.2 K-mean analysis

Source: Own study based on the data from Eurostat (2021)

intensity than countries in cluster 1. Higher PM_{10} exposure is linked to higher emissions, specific weather conditions (e.g., limited air circulation), or more reliance on PM_{10}-contributing factors (e.g., vehicle traffic, agriculture). The second cluster includes Bulgaria, Poland, and Estonia. The data for these countries are less clear. They have the highest levels of emission intensity and PM_{10} exposure. The variation between Poland, Bulgaria, and Estonia is engaging within this group. Poland and Bulgaria have terrible air pollution, while Estonia achieves excellent results.

Furthermore, the graph shows that countries in clusters 1 and 3 correlate more with each other than in cluster 2. Table 4.1 presents the basic statistics for the variables between 2014 and 2019 according to clusters for three groups.

Table 4.1 Basic statistics of variables according to clusters

	Group	n	Mean	Sd	Median	Min	Max	Skew	Kurtosis
X	First	79	235.6	65.99	236.97	107.75	364.31	−0.01	−0.84
	Second	16	1090.39	210.87	1037.8	840.26	1483.22	0.64	−1.1
	Third	61	512.88	100.82	492.95	378.05	777.12	0.72	−0.11
Y	First	79	18.76	4.58	19.1	10	32.7	0.2	0.11
	Second	16	27.84	10.65	32.75	10.7	41.2	−0.59	−1.48
	Third	61	25.21	4.58	25.3	10.8	35.1	−0.07	0.65

Source: Own study based on the data from Eurostat (2021)

The first cluster has the lowest average air emission intensity (235.6) compared to other clusters. This cluster also has the lowest average exposure to air pollution (18.76). Both emission intensity and exposure show low standard deviations (Sd), indicating a tighter distribution of data points within this cluster. The skewness values for both variables are close to 0, suggesting a symmetrical distribution. Kurtosis values are also near 0 (X) or slightly positive (Y), implying an average or slightly peaked distribution. According to CO_2 emission intensities and air emissions, the worst result in the first group was achieved in Portugal. In this group, the minimum emission intensity was achieved in Sweden (107.75) in 2019, but a minimum of PM_{10} – Finland in 2017.

The second cluster has the highest average air emission intensity (1090.39) and the highest average exposure to air pollution (27.84). The Sd are lower than the first and third clusters, indicating a tighter data distribution. The skewness for X is positive (0.64), suggesting a slight positive skew (more data points towards lower values). Kurtosis harms both variables, indicating a flatter distribution than a standard curve. According to both variables, Bulgaria reached the worst result.

The third cluster has an intermediate average air emission intensity (512.88) compared to the other two. This cluster also has intermediate average exposure to air pollution (25.21). The standard deviations are higher than the first clusters due to CO_2 emissions, indicating a more spread-out distribution of data points. However, it is similar to cluster 1 in terms of air pollution. The skewness for X is positive (0.72), suggesting a slight positive skew. Kurtosis for X is close to 0, while positive for Y (0.65), implying a slightly peaked distribution.

It is worth answering the question: Which factors determine the advantage of countries in cluster 1 (leaders) over cluster 3 (second rates) and two (marauders)? Understanding these determinants is essential for effective policy development and implementation aimed at mitigating air pollution. By identifying critical determinants of air quality and implementing targeted measures, the EU can continue to improve air quality standards and safeguard public health for current and future generations.

Renewable energy is one of the most critical factors in the EU's transformation towards good air quality. An attractive solution is proposed by Pyk, pointing to microgrids as a tool that not only enables the improvement of distributed renewable energy sources but also facilitates responsible business management in terms of environmental performance, mainly focusing on the innovation of these solutions (Pyk, 2023, p. 116). The development of microgrids responds to the needs of the EU, as one of the pillars of the energy transition is the development of civic energy (Kostecka-Jurczyk & Marak, 2024, p. 157).

Renewable energy technologies are crucial in mitigating air pollution through several mechanisms. Unlike fossil fuel combustion, renewable energy sources produce minimal or zero emissions of air pollutants such as sulphur dioxide (SO_2), nitrogen oxides (NO_x), particulate matter (PM), and greenhouse gases (GHGs). It provides a substitution effect because deploying renewable energy displaces fossil fuel-based power generation, reducing emissions of pollutants associated with conventional energy production. In addition to reducing air pollution, renewable energy deployment can yield co-benefits such as improved public health, enhanced energy security, and economic development. The direct benefit to the citizens of installing renewable energy should be a key element of national policy.

Comparing the share of renewable energy in final energy use across these countries reveals a range of progress. Frontrunners are Sweden (66.002%) and Finland (47.886%), with over half of their final energy consumption from renewables. Latvia (43.316%) and Denmark (41.602%) are also notable for their high shares. These countries have robust policies and resources to support renewable energy development. The EU's goal is to increase the share of renewable energy in final energy consumption to at least 42.5%, up from the previous 32% target, with the aspiration to reach 45% (European Parliament and the Council of the European Union, 2023), and these mentioned countries are close to expected outcomes. Several European nations like Estonia (38.472%), Austria (33.758%), and Portugal (34.677%) show substantial use of renewable energy sources, which are near to the goals from 2021. Other countries such as Croatia (27.924%), Lithuania (29.599%), Romania (24.140%), Slovenia (25.002%), Greece (22.678), Germany (20.796%), France (20.259%) are in the halfway. On the other hand, countries like Belgium (13.759%), Bulgaria (19.095%), Czechia (18.195%), Ireland (13.107), Italy (19.006%), the Netherlands (14.972%), Poland (16.879%), Hungary (15.190%), Slovakia (17.501%), Luxembourg (14.356), and Malta (13.404%) have a lower share of renewables in their final energy mix. They are earlier adopting renewable energy sources or have geographical limitations (Eurostat, 2022).

An essential factor distinguishing green transformation leaders is using new technologies for energy production. Traditional energy usage, often reliant on fossil fuels such as coal, oil, and natural gas, has significantly contributed to air pollution due to SO_2, NO_x, and PM emissions. These pollutants can harm air quality, human health, and the environment, leading to respiratory diseases, smog formation, and acid rain. New technologies aimed at improving the effectiveness of air quality focus on reducing emissions from energy production and transportation and enhancing monitoring and mitigation efforts. Some countries have favourable conditions for energy production through photovoltaics, while others use wind, hydro, or biogas. Countries should specialize in the energy production they perform best, which can bring them an advantage in achieving air quality standards. Political readiness can be crucial, as the EU has the geographical and technological potential to allow it to become independent from external raw materials. In light of the literature, technological innovations are one of the most exciting areas which have improved people's ability to manage energy supplies (Chen et al., 2021; Elia et al., 2021; Miao et al., 2018). Scientists explore the technological mix of renewable energy sources across EU member states. Solar (Luan et al., 2021), wind (Odam & De Vries, 2020), hydro (Blakers et al., 2021), and biomass (Costa et al., 2020) are standard technologies, but the balance differs significantly. They examine the factors driving these choices and their environmental and economic implications. Also, grid integration and energy storage are recurring topics in the literature (Abdalla et al., 2021). In articles, scientists investigate the challenges of integrating intermittent renewables into existing energy grids and the role of energy storage technologies in ensuring a stable energy supply.

The diverse landscape of solar thermal collectors' surface areas across European countries is influenced by geographical, climatic, economic, and policy factors. Countries with more prominent solar thermal collectors' surface areas, such as Germany, Spain, Italy, and Greece, typically have higher solar energy potential due to their geographical location and climatic conditions, making them favourable for solar energy utilization. On the other hand, Northern European countries like Denmark, Sweden, and Finland have relatively smaller surface areas for solar thermal collectors due to their higher latitudes, resulting in fewer daylight hours and less intense solar radiation than southern European countries. Due to climatic conditions (i.e., average annual temperatures higher than $13°C$), countries such as Spain, Italy, Greece, Portugal, Malta, Croatia, Bulgaria, Cyprus, and Malta seem to not benefit from their potential sufficiently. Even in countries with lower average temperatures, such as Germany, the Netherlands, Austria, and Poland, photovoltaic panels can still be viable thanks to technological developments, government support, and falling installation costs. The presence of supportive policies, incentives, and subsidies for renewable energy development can influence the adoption of solar thermal technology. Countries like Germany, Austria, and Denmark are known for their strong support of renewable energy, and they have significant surface areas dedicated to solar thermal collectors. The surface area of solar thermal collectors can also be influenced by population density and urbanization patterns. Countries with higher population densities and urban areas may have less space for solar installations (Eurostat, 2024f).

The technology also meets the needs of those countries where the ability to use solar energy is not as efficient. Countries can use wind or hydro, for example, to produce energy. Wind energy uses the kinetic energy of the wind to turn the blades of wind turbines, which generate electricity through generators. Wind is a renewable energy source because it is an endless resource, and its use does not produce GHG emissions or air pollution. Wind power plants can be installed on land or at sea, and their efficiency depends on several factors, such as wind speed, location, and technology. Hydropower harnesses the kinetic and potential energy of flowing or falling water in rivers, streams, or reservoirs. Hydroelectric power plants have water turbines that turn when water flows through them, driving electric generators. Hydropower is also a renewable energy source that does not emit GHG or cause air pollution. Types of hydropower plants include pumped storage plants, run-of-river plants, and tidal and tidal power plants.

Significant variations across the region can be observed comparing the wind electricity production capacities among EU countries in 2022. Malta and Slovakia have the lowest wind electricity production capacities, with Malta having the smallest capacity at 0.100 units. Several countries, such as Slovenia, Cyprus, Latvia, Bulgaria, Lithuania, and Hungary, have relatively limited wind electricity production capacities. These countries may have challenges or limited resources for wind energy development. Countries like Czechia, Estonia, and Croatia have moderate wind electricity production capacities, indicating some investment and development in wind energy infrastructure. Moving up the scale, there are countries with higher wind electricity production capacities, such as Romania, Portugal, Ireland, and Greece. These countries have invested more significantly in wind energy and have larger capacities to generate electricity from wind sources. Belgium, Finland, Denmark, Netherlands, France, Italy, Poland, Spain, Sweden, and Germany are among the top performers in wind electricity production capacities. These countries have made substantial investments in wind energy infrastructure and have favourable conditions for wind power generation (Eurostat, 2024b).

The use of wind and hydroelectric power to generate electricity is becoming increasingly popular, as these technologies are greener and cost-competitive compared to traditional energy sources such as fossil fuels. Appropriate investment, technology development, and a suitable regulatory framework can promote the development of these forms of renewable energy in many countries. Also, the role of hydropower in the EU energy landscape is significant, contributing to electricity generation, energy security, and air quality goals. It influences the diversity of the EU's energy mix, complementing other renewable energy sources such as wind, solar, and biomass. Its reliability and ability to provide baseload and dispatchable power make it an essential component of the overall energy system, particularly in regions with abundant water resources. Hydroelectric power plants use the potential energy of water to turn turbines, which means they emit no gaseous or dust pollution. It is one of the oldest and most established renewable energy sources. Hydropower plants utilize the kinetic energy of flowing water to generate electricity, providing a reliable and continuous power source.

Malta and Cyprus have no reported electricity production capacity for hydro in 2022. Due to geography, Denmark has a low capacity of 6.644 units, with fewer suitable sites for hydroelectric installations. Several countries have moderate hydroelectric capacity, including Belgium, Hungary, the Netherlands, Estonia, and Ireland. Countries like Austria, Spain, France, Italy, and Sweden have notable hydroelectric capacity, indicating substantial investment in hydroelectric infrastructure and utilization of available water resources. Sweden, France, Italy, Spain, and Austria rank among the top performers in hydroelectric capacity, with significant contributions to the EU's overall hydroelectric generation. Overall, the data highlights the varied landscape of hydroelectric capacity across EU countries, influenced by factors such as geography, water resources, and investment in infrastructure (Eurostat, 2024b).

Technology also makes it possible to solve the air quality problem in connection with the need to heat or cool households. Heat pumps use electricity to transfer heat from one location to another, rather than burning fossil fuels directly. This reduces the emission of pollutants such as SO_2, NO_x, PM, and GHGs associated with conventional heating systems powered by coal, oil, or natural gas. Heat pumps are highly efficient systems that provide heating and cooling functions. By extracting heat from outdoor air, water, or the ground and transferring it indoors during colder months and vice versa during warmer months, heat pumps can maintain comfortable indoor temperatures without relying on combustion processes that contribute to air pollution. It can be powered by renewable energy sources such as wind, solar, and hydroelectric power. Utilizing clean energy to operate heat pump systems further reduces the environmental impact associated with heating and cooling processes, contributing to improved air quality.

There is significant variation in installed thermal capacity among European countries, with Italy, France, and Spain leading in the volume of heat pumps. Southern European countries have higher installed capacities compared to Northern European countries. However, it should be remembered that heat pumps cannot be the most effective solution during the winter period, when the temperatures fall below 0 degrees, and there is a lack of rays from the Sun. For instance, even though the air quality in Sweden is good, higher pollution levels do occur during the cold winter periods. NO_x and PM levels rise due to combustion during the winter (Smart City Sweden, 2024). Overall, the analysis suggests that while some European countries have made significant strides in adopting heat pump technology, there are still opportunities for expansion and improvement, especially in regions with lower capacities (Eurostat, 2024c).

It is worth noting that the three technologies under discussion related to the operation of the renewable energy market (heat pumps, solar panels, and windmills) can be used in both manufacturing enterprises and households. They can, therefore, complement state-level efforts. It should be noted that there are several significant barriers to applying these technologies, which may differentiate the energy potential of EU countries. First, photovoltaic and heat pumps can require a significant financial outlay for purchase and installation, which can be a barrier for individuals or companies with limited budgets. Second, many individuals and businesses are unaware of the benefits of heat pumps, windmills, and solar panels and do not understand how these devices work or the potential energy savings. In addition, in some geographic areas, especially in densely urbanized cities, finding a suitable site for installing heat pumps can be difficult, which can be a technical barrier. Heat pumps require adjustments to heating systems. In some cases, installing a heat pump may require a change or adjustment to the heating system, which can increase costs and make adapting this technology more complex. Overcoming these barriers requires coordinated action at the national and European levels, such as public education, financial support for the installation of energy-efficient technologies, standardization of regulations, and the development of appropriate infrastructure and support services for users (Oryani et al., 2021 pp. 971–983; Pasqualetti, 2011, pp. 201–223; Sen & Ganguly, 2017, pp. 1170–1181).

Another essential instrument of green change is liquid biofuels. Their production can also contribute to local economies by supporting agriculture and the biofuel industry, but cannot be used in households. Biofuels are fuels produced or derived from organic materials such as plants, organic waste, or biomass. They can be an alternative to fossil fuels such as oil, coal, or natural gas. There are several types of biofuels, including liquid biofuels (such as biodiesel), gaseous biofuels (such as biogas) and solid biofuels (such as wood pellets). The primary function of biofuels is to replace fossil fuels to reduce GHG emissions, reduce air pollution, and reduce dependence on imported energy resources. Through the use of biofuels, the negative environmental impact of the transportation, industrial, and energy sectors can be reduced, helping to improve air quality and reduce carbon emissions, which has a positive impact on the fight against climate change. In addition, biofuels can be produced from organic waste, which contributes to their efficient disposal and reduces the amount of waste going to landfills.

As mentioned above, renewable energy sources such as solar, wind, and hydro, the landscape of liquid biofuel production capacities in Europe is also diverse, influenced by factors such as industrial development, policy frameworks, agricultural resources, and environmental considerations. Countries with well-established industrial sectors tend to have higher production capacities. For instance, Germany, Spain, France, Italy, the Netherlands, and

Poland have high capacities due to their advanced industrial infrastructure and intense focus on renewable energy. The presence or absence of supportive policies and incentives for renewable energy production can significantly impact a country's biofuel production capacity. Countries like Germany and Spain, which have implemented supportive policies for renewable energy, tend to have higher capacities. Agricultural resources and practices are crucial in determining biofuel production capacities. Countries with significant agricultural sectors, such as Poland and France, have higher capacities due to feedstock availability for biofuel production. Also, countries that have invested in research and development of biofuel technologies and infrastructure have higher capacities. This is evident in countries like Germany and Sweden, which have been at the forefront of renewable energy innovation (Eurostat, 2024d)

An essential element of the Green Deal is transport. This sector accounts for about 20% of CO_2 production and causes a high burden on air quality (especially in European cities). Increasing public interest in electric and hybrid cars can significantly contribute to achieving EU targets. Such measures will address several issues, including reducing the use of fossil fuels and emissions of harmful substances, i.e. GHG and air pollution. Significant variations among countries are occurring in the adoption of new zero-emission vehicles. Some countries, such as Sweden, the Netherlands, and Denmark, have notably higher shares, indicating a more muscular uptake of zero-emission vehicles within their respective automotive markets. On the other hand, countries like Slovakia, Czechia, and Greece have relatively lower shares, suggesting a slower adoption rate of zero-emission vehicles in those regions (Eurostat, 2024e).

Factors influencing these differences may include government incentives, infrastructure development, consumer preferences, and the availability of zero-emission vehicle models within each country. Economic factors and cultural attitudes towards sustainability and air quality concerns may also shape the adoption of zero-emission vehicles across different nations. The main problem in developing this area of the economy is the number of charging stations for electric cars. According to data from the European Automobile Manufacturers Association (ACEA), most EU member states severely lack electric charging points on the road network. Most charging stations in the EU are concentrated in just a few countries, despite those countries making up a small portion of the EU's land area. This uneven distribution is stark – the Netherlands, for example, has far more chargers than Romania, even though Romania is much more significant. This lack of balanced infrastructure likely plays a role in EV sales, as countries with more charging stations tend also to have higher EV adoption rates (European Automobile Manufacturers Association, 2024).

The European Court of Auditors is not satisfied with the degree of implementation of electric car charging systems. The main problems highlighted by the Court are the uniform plug standard, the availability of charging stations depending on the country, and the lack of harmonization of payment systems. Without a comprehensive infrastructure gap analysis, the Commission could not ensure that EU funding goes where needed. The EU is still far from achieving the 1 million charging points target by 2025. The Court has, therefore, made several recommendations to the European Commission to improve the roll-out of publicly accessible charging infrastructure across the EU (European Court of Auditors, 2021). The lack of adequate facilities and infrastructure for recharging electric cars is a significant barrier to achieving the Green Deal targets, as residents of countries with poor charging infrastructure cannot be expected to opt for electric cars.

Although the decisive influence on air quality is the emissions and pollutants generated by the events and their effects on the environment, environmental disasters can indirectly affect air quality.

For example, forest fires can release large amounts of harmful substances into the atmosphere, such as smoke, soot, nitrogen, and sulphur. These substances can significantly degrade air quality and threaten human health. In addition, flooding can lead to the release of toxic chemicals from flooded industrial areas, landfills, or sewage systems. These pollutants can seep into surface water and soil and evaporate into the atmosphere, negatively affecting air quality. Another example is severe ecosystem damage, which can affect natural processes such as air filtration and water purification. Violating these processes can contribute to the deterioration of air quality in affected areas.

The analysed indicator of climate-related economic losses by type of event mainly refers to the analysis of economic losses caused by events related to climate change, such as floods, droughts, hurricanes, or fires. It makes it possible to show the scale of the problems countries face where the indicated disasters occur.

The EU Green Deal recognizes climate change leads to economic losses across different sectors. These losses can result from extreme weather events such as floods, storms, heatwaves, droughts, and wildfires, as well as slow-onset events like sea-level rise and changes in precipitation patterns. Each type of event poses unique challenges to economic sectors, infrastructure, and communities. In literature, most studies have focused on single or limited hazards and explained the consequences of climate extremes (Arnell et al., 2013, pp. 512–519; Piontek et al., 2014, pp. 3233–3238). However, one must realize that the cognition of climate-related economic losses by type of event for the EU Green Deal involves understanding the various ways in which climate change impacts the economy, categorizing these impacts by event type, and developing strategies to mitigate and adapt to these challenges within the framework of the EU Green Deal. Forzieri tries to predict that "damages could triple by the 2020s, multiply six-fold by mid-century, and amount to more than ten times present damage of €3.4 billion per year by the end of the century due only to climate change". (Forzieri et al., 2018, p. 97).

There are significant differences in the scale of economic losses among EU countries. For example, Germany consistently experienced some of the highest losses, followed by Italy and Belgium. Germany experienced substantial losses in 2018 and 2022, while other countries, such as Belgium and Spain, had peaks in 2021. An indicator related to losses due to climate change explains the difference in the Green Deal Factor. Although the indicator in Belgium remained at an average of 1.5 between 2013 and 2020, due to losses in 2021, Belgium scored 0 points. On the other hand, countries like Estonia, Malta, and Finland seem to have minimal to no reported losses during this period. Some countries show consistent trends over the years. For instance, France experienced increasing losses from 2013 to 2018, followed by a slight decrease in 2019 and 2020 before increasing again in 2021 and 2022. This could indicate a need for enhanced resilience measures in the face of climate change (Eurostat, 2024a).

In summarizing the above considerations, it should be noted that countries achieving successes related to improving air quality have been highly active in transforming energy sources from traditional to renewable. Sweden is a leader in renewable energy sources and can also be an example for other EU countries in producing energy from water or wind. In addition, it is a leader in the use of zero-emission vehicles. Among the countries that use new technologies to produce clean energy, Italy, France, Spain, and Germany are also leaders in achieving good results in wind, solar, and hydro energy production. At the same time, they belong to cluster 1, which achieved the lowest CO_2 emissions and caused the least air pollution.

4.2 Lessons learnt from the implementation of air quality legislation at countries level

Air pollution poses significant risks to human health, ecosystems, and the global climate. In response to the Green Deal, the EU countries have developed and implemented air quality legislation to mitigate pollution sources and protect public health. Implementing such legislation has been accompanied by various experiences, challenges, and lessons learned. As indicated in Chapter 3, the EU consistently implements policies to reduce air pollution, improving year after year. It is, therefore, worth examining whether the EU's efforts to reduce air pollution are improving the health of the EU population and reducing mortality associated with air pollution. It is worth remembering that while there are some successes for the EU, it is apparent that the goals the EU is setting are not yet realised and require further investment and action.

Air pollution is now recognized as a significant global public health risk factor causing premature death. It consists of various substances, such as $PM_{2.5}$, PM_{10} particulate matter, NO_x, SO_x, benzene, formaldehyde, dioxins, and many other toxic chemicals. Air pollution leads to various diseases of civilization through various mechanisms of action on the human body.

Particulate matter (e.g., $PM_{2.5}$ and PM_{10}) and chemicals in polluted air can be inhaled by humans and deposited in the lungs. This can lead to airway irritation, pneumonia, chronic obstructive pulmonary disease (COPD) and asthma exacerbations. Long-term exposure to air pollution can lead to lung damage and reduced lung function. Inhalation of polluted air not only affects the human respiratory system but also causes cardiovascular diseases such as heart attack, stroke, hypertension and coronary artery disease. Chemicals in the air can affect the cardiovascular system through oxidative stress, inflammation and blood vessel dysfunction. A dangerous consequence of airborne chemicals such as benzene and dioxins are cancers: lung cancer, laryngeal cancer, bladder cancer, and other cancers of the respiratory and digestive systems. Studies suggest that exposure to air pollution may be associated with a higher risk of developing neurological diseases such as Alzheimer's disease, dementia, neurological disorders in children, and depression. The metallic particles in polluted air may be particularly harmful, as they can penetrate the brain and cause neurological damage. In addition, there is evidence that air pollution may be associated with an increased risk of obesity, type 2 diabetes, and metabolic syndrome. Mechanisms for this association may include the effects of pollution on inflammatory responses, insulin resistance, and lipid and glucose metabolism (Boogaard et al., 2019, p. 417; Brunekreef & Holgate, 2002, pp. 1233–1242; Katsouyanni, 2003, pp. 143–156; Schwela, 2000, pp. 13–42).

All these mechanisms of action of air pollution can lead to various diseases of civilization by damaging various systems and organs in the human body, eventually contributing to premature death. Epidemiological studies have shown a link between exposure to air pollution and an increased risk of premature death. It is estimated that annual exposure to elevated concentrations of air pollutants can lead to a shortened life span of several months or even several years, especially in the elderly and those with existing health conditions. People live with diseases related to exposure to air pollution; this is a burden in terms of personal suffering and significant costs to the healthcare sector (Barwick et al., 2024, pp. 1–52). The European Environmental Agency (EEA) published the report *Health Risk Assessment of Air Pollution: Assessing the Environmental Burden of Disease in Europe in 2021*, which presents the results of the environmental burden of disease (EBD) assessment related to air pollution in 2021 for the 27 member states of the EU (European Environment Agency, 2023a).

The report presents the findings of the assessment of the EBD linked to air pollution in 2021 across the 27 member states of the EU and an additional 14 European countries, including Albania, Andorra, Bosnia and Herzegovina, Iceland, Kosovo under UNSCR 1244/99, Liechtenstein, Monaco, Montenegro, North Macedonia, Norway, San Marino, Serbia, Switzerland, and Türkiye. The assessment focuses on three key pollutants: delicate particulate matter ($PM_{2.5}$), nitrogen dioxide (NO_2), and ozone (O_3), considering their impact on both all-cause mortality and cause-specific mortality and morbidity. Various indicators of the burden of disease were utilised for the analysis, including attributable deaths (AD), years of life lost (YLL), years lived with disability (YLD), disability-adjusted life years (DALY), and attributable hospitalization cases.

In 2021, prolonged exposure to $PM_{2.5}$ and NO_2 concentrations exceeding the World Health Organization (WHO) Air Quality Guideline levels led to 293,000 and 69,000 ADs from all natural causes, respectively, while short-term exposure to O_3 resulted in 27,000 ADs. Specifically, for the EU27, the numbers were 253,000, 52,000, *and* 22,000, respectively. When considering both the number of deaths and the age at which they occur, the YLL per 100,000 inhabitants for long-term exposure to $PM_{2.5}$ and NO_2 were 2,936,000 (618) and 740,000 (132), respectively, and 299,000 (54) for short-term exposure to O_3. For the EU27, the YLL per 100,000 inhabitants were 2,584,000 (584), 532,000 (120), *and* 234,000 (53), respectively. In terms of long-term exposure, both all-cause and cause-specific analyses indicate that $PM_{2.5}$ is the pollutant with the highest burden. Cause-specific analyses revealed 2,528,363 DALY for all countries or 2,310,387 DALY for the EU27 attributable to $PM_{2.5}$. In contrast, the burden attributable to NO_2 was notably lower, with 634,721 DALY for all countries and 403,788 DALY for the EU27. Ischemic heart disease contributed the most to the overall burden of $PM_{2.5}$, with 759,303 DALY for all countries and 704,525 DALY for the EU27. In contrast, the lowest burden was associated with asthma (children), with 25,932 *and* 23,969 DALY for all countries and the EU27, respectively. For NO_2, diabetes mellitus had the highest disease burden (314,574 DALY for all countries; *EU27*: 197,031 DALY), whereas asthma (adults) had the lowest (all countries: 115,425 DALY; EU27: 62,460 DALY). No corresponding indicators were calculated for O_3, but short-term exposure to O_3 was linked to 15,986 attributable hospital admissions in the selected European countries. It is important to note that different age groups (children, adults, and elderly) were considered in the estimates based on relevant concentration-response functions. (European Environment Agency, 2023a).

It is worth analysing how premature mortality from air pollution has changed in the EU. Premature death attributable to exposure to delicate PM allows monitoring of the effects of air pollution on public health. It assesses the effectiveness of measures to improve air quality and reduce air-related deaths. In 2005, there were 431.114 premature deaths attributed to exposure to delicate PM. From 2007 to 2011, there was a general trend of increasing premature deaths, reaching a peak of 392,315 in 2011. From 2012 to 2019, there has been a change in the trend, and the EU has begun to record progress in reducing premature mortality caused by pollution. By 2019, the number of premature deaths decreased to 231,286. Unfortunately, some fluctuations in this regard can be observed in recent years. In 2020 and 2021, premature deaths increased slightly compared to the previous years but remained lower than the peak in 2011. The target for premature deaths in 2030, according to the Zero Pollution Action Plan, is 194,001. Overall, the data indicates that there has been some progress in reducing premature deaths attributable to exposure to delicate PM over the years, with a notable decrease from the peak in 2011 to 2019. However, there is still room for improvement in reaching the target set for 2030. Therefore, the EU should respond appropriately to reduce the impact of harmful substances on human health in individual countries. Continued efforts to implement pollution reduction measures and improve air quality will be crucial in achieving this goal (European Environment Agency, 2023b).

According to European Environment Agency, if the trend seen in the past ten years were to continue, the decline in premature mortality attributable to $PM_{2.5}$ would reach 68% by 2030 (from 2005 levels), i.e., there will be an overachievement of the 55% zero pollution reduction target (European Environment Agency, 2023b). The zero pollution action plan target is set at the EU level, but looking at the change in the mortality due to exposure to $PM_{2.5}$ at the country level is helpful. Figure 4.3 depicts the estimated number of premature deaths per 100,000 inhabitants attributable to exposure to annual $PM_{2.5}$ concentrations above 5 μg/m^3 in 2005 and 2021.

Figure 4.3 compares premature deaths attributable to exposure to PM2.5 at the country level in 2005 and 2021 for European countries and the EU. The data suggests an overall positive trend in reducing premature deaths attributable to PM2.5 exposure across Europe, reflecting efforts to improve air quality and public health over the past decade and a half.

Most countries have experienced decreased premature deaths attributable to PM2.5 exposure from 2005 to 2021. This indicates progress in addressing air pollution and improving public health. While some countries have significantly reduced premature deaths, others have experienced smaller declines or even increases in mortality. For instance, although Bulgaria,

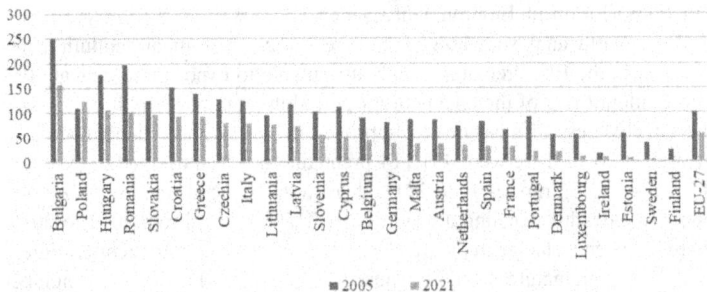

Figure 4.3 Premature deaths attributable to exposure to PM2.5

Source: Own study based on the data from European Environment Agency (2023b)

Romania, and Hungary show a decrease, they still have a higher number of premature deaths than other countries in 2005 and 2021. Poland experienced a slight increase in premature deaths from 2005 to 2021, suggesting ongoing challenges in these countries. Some countries stand out for their substantial reductions in premature deaths attributable to $PM_{2.5}$ exposure. These include Czechia, Italy, Lithuania, Latvia, Slovenia, Cyprus, Belgium, Germany, Malta, Austria, the Netherlands, Spain, France, Portugal, Denmark, Luxembourg, Ireland, Estonia, Sweden, Finland, and the EU. Countries like Estonia, Sweden, and Finland have achieved impressive reductions, with single-digit figures in 2021, indicating effective air quality management measures. There are noticeable differences in premature mortality rates across different regions of Europe. Southern and Eastern European countries have higher rates than Western and Northern European countries. Countries like Poland, Bulgaria, Romania, Hungary, and Croatia still face relatively high levels of premature deaths compared to their Western European counterparts. This means that most European countries have done their homework and taken appropriate action to reduce air pollution.

It is essential to acknowledge that air pollution exposure does not affect all populations equally within EU countries and other parts of the world. It often leads to marginalized communities bearing a disproportionate burden of environmental injustice. Socio-economic factors like income, education, and race/ethnicity play a significant role in determining exposure levels and susceptibility to the health impacts of air pollution. Those residing in low-income neighbourhoods and minority communities are more likely to inhabit areas with elevated air pollution levels, often due to their proximity to industrial facilities, busy roads, and limited access to green spaces. These environmental disparities worsen health inequities, amplifying preexisting socio-economic disparities in health outcomes.

Table 4.2 presents the population-attributable fraction (PAF) for mortality attributable to the joint effects of Household Air Pollution (HAP) and Ambient Air Pollution (AAP) in 2016, categorized by WHO regions and specific diseases. In low- and middle-income countries (LMIC) in Africa, South-East Asia, the Western Pacific, and the Eastern Mediterranean, HAP and AAP contribute significantly to mortality across all diseases, with exceptionally high PAFs for ALRI. In high-income countries (HIC) in Africa, the PAFs are lower than LMICs but still considerable for ALRI and COPD. HICs in the Western Pacific show lower but noticeable PAFs, while the situation is the opposite in the Eastern Mediterranean. Similarly to Africa, America's LMICs exhibit higher PAFs than HICs across all diseases, albeit lower than in Africa. PAFs for ALRI and COPD are notable in both LMICs and HICs. In Europe, both LMICs and HICs show relatively lower PAFs than other regions (World Health Organization, 2018).

Overall, the European results indicate that LMICs and HICs in the region experience less attributable mortality due to air pollution than in

Table 4.2 Population-attributable fraction for mortality attributable to the joint effects of HAP and AAP in 2016 by region and disease

WHO region	ALI Acute lower respiratory disease	COPD Chronic obstructive pulmonary disease	Lung cancer	IHD Ischemic heart disease	Stroke
Africa LMIC	64%	55%	39%	38%	36%
Africa HIC	19%	16%	14%	16%	13%
America LMIC	25%	23%	16%	18%	14%
America HIC	8%	9%	4%	9%	7%
Eastern Mediterranean LMIC	54%	46%	30%	28%	26%
Eastern Mediterranean HIC	42%	37%	31%	26%	22%
Europe LMIC	22%	22%	15%	15%	12%
Europe HIC	12%	13%	8%	11%	9%
South-East Asia LMIC	61%	57%	50%	38%	33%
Western Pacific LMIC	52%	50%	45%	29%	27%
Western Pacific HIC	13%	14%	9%	11%	9%
HICs	12%	12%	7%	11%	9%
LMICs	56%	50%	39%	29%	27%
World	50%	43%	29%	25%	24%

LMIC: Low- and middle-income
HIC: High-income

Source: (World Health Organization, 2018)

other parts of the Globe, with LMICs facing relatively higher burdens. This highlights the importance of continued efforts to address air quality and mitigate the health impacts of air pollution across all income levels in Europe. While the specific PAFs vary across regions and income levels, the data underscores the substantial impact of both HAP and AAP on mortality, with LMICs bearing a disproportionately higher burden (World Health Organization, 2018).

In conclusion, air pollution represents a significant public health challenge in EU countries, with adverse effects on respiratory health, cardiovascular health, and overall mortality. Addressing this complex issue requires a multifaceted approach, integrating scientific research, policy development, and public engagement. By implementing evidence-based interventions to reduce emissions, mitigate exposure, and protect vulnerable populations, EU countries can work towards achieving sustainable development goals and safeguarding the health and well-being of present and future generations. Collaboration among governments, researchers, healthcare professionals, and civil society stakeholders is essential to effectively address the impacts of air pollution on public health and promote environmental justice across diverse communities.

4.3 Good practices for reducing air pollution in European countries

Nowadays, air pollution is one of the most severe health and environmental problems we face worldwide. Using the best practices allows the implementation of the EU's Green Deal strategy. Sweden is an excellent example of how it is possible to reduce the effects of premature deaths. Due to joint efforts, clear air may be the success of all EU countries, not only the leaders of the Green Deal. To this end, countries judged as marauders or second-rated should use solutions applied by the best countries, such as Sweden, Denmark, Italy, and Germany. In this part of the book, one will take a closer look at selected pollution reduction policies applied by European leaders.

Recognizing the urgency of addressing air pollution as a public health priority, selected EU countries have implemented various policy responses and interventions to reduce emissions, improve air quality, and protect public health. These initiatives include regulatory measures such as:

- investment in public transportation infrastructure, urban planning strategies to reduce traffic congestion,
- emission standards for vehicles and industrial sources,
- promotion of cleaner technologies,
- public awareness campaigns.

Investing in public transportation is the most effective way to reduce city pollution. Building new subways, streetcars, and train lines, and upgrading existing public transportation infrastructure will help reduce the use of individual cars, reducing harmful emissions. For example, Luxembourg is the first country in Europe to introduce completely free public transportation. In February 2020, the government decided to abolish fares on all buses, trains, and streetcars in the country, and implementation of this reform began in January 2021. For now, Luxembourg is the only European country that has introduced free public transportation. However, several other countries, such as Iceland, Norway, and Estonia, also offer free public transportation in specific regions or for certain groups of people. Introducing free public transportation in Luxembourg is part of a broader government plan to improve air quality and reduce pollution. In February 2021, the government also established a new fuel tax tariff to encourage the use of public transportation and EVs (Government of the Grand Duchy of Luxembourg, 2024).

However, Sweden is the EU country that has introduced the most ambitious emission reduction targets, resulting in Europe's best air pollution performance. Sweden plans to achieve climate neutrality by 2045. To this end, the country is investing in renewable energy sources, such as solar and wind power, and more energy-efficient technologies. It promotes sustainable transportation and invests in public transportation and bicycle infrastructure.

Bicycle transportation in Sweden is well-developed and popular. In 2019, the number of cyclists in Sweden was about 2.2 million, accounting for about 20% of all trips. Sweden has an extensive bicycle path network connecting cities, villages, and other important places. The paths are usually well-marked and well-maintained, and their width allows for safe riding.

In Sweden, bicycles can be carried on regional trains. In Skåne, this is the Skanetraffiken network, which has over 1,000 bicycle stations. In many European cities, renting bicycles by the minute is also possible. Special city bikes can also be rented for free for short periods. Sweden ranked second in the WHO ranking of bicycle-friendly countries in 2017. Sweden scored 79 points out of a possible 100, placing it second behind the Netherlands. It is a country with great potential for bicycle transportation. Many bicycle paths, wide roads, and friendly regulations make cycling safe and convenient. In addition, thanks to an extensive network of regional trains, bicycle travel is possible even over long distances (Visit Sweden, 2024). By drawing on good practices, countries can invest in infrastructure that reduces air pollution. Building new public transportation lines, developing a network of bicycle paths, or promoting electric modes of transportation are some measures that can reduce air pollution from traffic.

Another way to improve green infrastructure can be through various types of support. EU countries are promoting the electrification of transportation through financial incentives, tax breaks, and infrastructure for EVs. EVs emit significantly less pollution than those powered by traditional internal combustion engines. In certain nations, cyclists are even financially incentivized. For instance, various businesses in the Netherlands offer tax credits amounting to ¬0.19 per kilometre ridden. Similarly, in Bari, Italy, cyclists receive ¬0.21 per kilometre for commuting to work, capped at ¬25 monthly, and the local government extends support by contributing up to ¬155 towards purchasing a new bicycle. Moreover, multinational corporations worldwide are increasingly adapting their services to address environmental concerns, particularly emphasizing sustainability. Uber Technologies, Inc., for instance, made a notable shift in 2018, redirecting its focus from traditional taxis to electric bikes and scooters. Additionally, Uber invested $170 million in the electric scooter company Lime in 2020. An exciting example is Swedish Volvo, whose priorities include efforts to reduce air pollution through the introduction of autonomous and electric solutions. According to them, quieter, electric city rubbish trucks operating at night at low speeds will improve air quality through zero NO_x and particulate emissions, improve energy use, reduce congestion and significantly lower noise levels. The fill rate of trucks currently averages only $40 - 50\%$ of the total payload. Sharing economy business models, artificial intelligence, and machine learning may optimize the flow of goods, reduce transportation needs, and save precious natural resources (Volvo, 2024). This means that the value of transportation can be doubled without increasing the number of trucks on the road.

Some EU countries are investing in intelligent traffic management systems and other technologies that reduce the need for traditional modes of transportation and emissions. Intelligent traffic management systems (ITS) use information and communications technology (ICT) to optimize traffic flow and improve safety. They include traffic management centres that monitor traffic in real time and adjust traffic signals to minimize congestion and delays. In addition, they use traveller information systems that provide drivers with information about road conditions, detours, and alternative modes of transportation. No less critical tasks can be performed by solutions with parking management. They help find free parking spaces and reduce the traffic associated with searching for a parking space. For example, Stockholm in Sweden has introduced a tolling system that encourages drivers to avoid rush hour and use public transportation. This has resulted in a 25% reduction in traffic. In Helsinki, Finland, investment has been made in an extensive network of bicycle paths and a bicycle rental program, leading to a 20% increase in the proportion of bicycle trips. In Vienna, Paris, and Madrid, the traffic management system uses data from cameras, traffic sensors, and GPS to ensure a smooth traffic flow. The system is also linked to public transportation systems to ensure better coordination between different modes of transportation. In Poland, the possibility of changing cars into public transportation is famous in the largest cities such as Kraków and Warsaw, where traffic jams are one of the biggest problems.

Innovative transportation solutions offer several benefits, including reducing traffic jams and delays. ITS optimizes traffic flow, which reduces travel time and driver frustration. It also results in increased safety. ITS systems monitor traffic and warn drivers of hazards, helping prevent accidents. Intelligent traffic management and encouraging alternative modes of transportation help reduce emissions and improve air quality. The solutions indicated contribute to an improved quality of life. Less traffic congestion and pollution lead to a healthier and more pleasant environment for residents.

The revised EU law is expected to reduce air pollution in the EU, provide citizens with a clean and healthy environment, and achieve the goal of zero air pollution by 2050. The changes include new emission standards for new cars, trucks, and buses and the promotion of EVs and alternative fuels. In addition, the law includes an increased emphasis on creating better urban infrastructure that will reduce the need for cars and improve public mobility. There are currently more than 300 low-emission zones in Europe. Cities with low emission zones include Amsterdam, Berlin, Brussels, Dublin, Helsinki, Paris, Stockholm, and Vienna. The WHO recommends that all European cities introduce low-emission zones, as they effectively reduce air pollution. Low Emission Zones (LEZ) are areas in cities where high-emission vehicles are restricted or prohibited from entering. They are designed to improve air quality and reduce pollution. In Amsterdam, for example, the zone covers the city centre and part of the Zuidoost district. Diesel vehicles registered before

2001 and gasoline vehicles registered before 1992 are prohibited from entering the zone. In Berlin, the zone covers the city centre. Diesel vehicles registered before 2006 and gasoline vehicles registered before 1993 are prohibited from entering the zone. In Brussels, the zone covers the entire city. Diesel vehicles registered before 2001 and gasoline vehicles registered before 1997 are prohibited from entering the zone. As the examples show, different rules may apply to different types of vehicles in low-emission zones. For example, some cities may allow diesel vehicles that meet specific emission standards to enter. Low-emission zones are an effective way to improve air quality in cities. They can reduce air pollution, improve public health and make cities more pedestrian and bicycle-friendly, so countries should use these measures to reduce city pollution.

Many EU countries support low-carbon agriculture. Examples of such countries include France, Germany, and Poland. These countries offer various forms of support to farmers, including subsidies, loans, and tax breaks. This support encourages farmers to adopt sustainable farming practices, such as using organic fertilizers and cover crops. Such practices help reduce GHG emissions, improve soil quality, and increase biodiversity. Support for low-carbon agriculture is necessary because agriculture is one of the main economic sectors contributing to GHG emissions. Therefore, farmers need to use sustainable agricultural practices to reduce their emissions and contribute to the fight against climate change. In Germany, for example, the government offers farmers subsidies to purchase agricultural machinery that is more energy-efficient and environmentally friendly. The Polish government also offers farmers subsidies to purchase agricultural machinery that is more energy-efficient and environmentally friendly.

The development of new technologies in agriculture can help improve air quality in several ways, including improving fuel quality. Implementing stricter emission standards for motor vehicles and promoting alternative fuels, such as biofuels and hydrogen, helps reduce emissions. Biofuels are produced from plants such as corn, soybeans, and sugarcane and can replace fossil fuels. Hydrogen is an emission-free fuel that can be produced from various sources, including natural gas and water.

Another way is by reducing emissions from animal farming. Animal farming is a significant source of methane and ammonia emissions, contributing to air pollution. New technologies, such as improved feed management and feed additives, can help reduce these emissions. Biogas plants also play an essential role in reducing air pollution by converting organic waste into animal manure, crop waste, and food industry waste into biogas. Biogas is a renewable energy source that can produce electricity, heat, or transportation fuel. Biogas production in biogas plants has many environmental benefits, including reducing methane emissions and other air pollutants and improving air quality. Methane is a potent GHG that contributes to climate change. Biogas plants capture and use methane that would otherwise be released into the atmosphere. Biogas plants also reduce emissions of other air pollutants, such as ammonia, hydrogen sulphide, and volatile organic compounds (VOCs). By reducing methane emissions and other air pollutants, biogas plants help improve air quality, bringing health benefits to people and the environment. Not to be overlooked is that biogas plants offer economic benefits in addition to environmental benefits. Biogas can be sold to the power grid or used to power industrial plants or households. They can also produce fertilizer, which can be used to improve soil fertility.

Implementing biogas plants is essential to reducing air pollution and protecting the environment. Biogas plants offer a sustainable solution to the problem of organic waste while contributing to producing renewable energy and improving air quality. An example of a biogas plant in Europe is the Biogas Plant in Holstebro, Denmark. It is one of the largest biogas plants in the world, and it processes organic waste from agriculture, the food industry, and households. The biogas plant produces biogas, which is used to generate electricity and heat. The biogas plant in Güssing, Austria, is the world's first biogas plant to power an entire municipality with electricity and heat. The biogas plant processes organic waste from agriculture and the food industry. The biogas plant in Malmoe, Sweden, is powered by household waste. The biogas plant produces biogas that are used to produce electricity and heat.

These examples show that biogas plants can reduce air pollution and produce renewable energy. As the technology develops and interest in sustainable solutions grows, more biogas plants can be expected to be built. They can perfectly complement other renewable energy production technologies, as they are not dependent on weather conditions like photovoltaic panels and wind power.

With industry being one of the most important economic sectors responsible for air pollution, it is essential to adapt EU standards to the state level. The EU is introducing strict emission standards for industry, especially for sectors such as power generation, steel, chemicals, and refining. Reducing emissions from these sources helps reduce the amount of dust in the air. Today, EU industrial emissions regulations are strict. They require industrial companies to reduce their emissions of air, water, and land pollutants. The regulations apply to all industries, including energy, metallurgy, chemicals, refineries, pulp and paper, metals, and ceramics. Over the past 40 years, industrial emissions in the EU have fallen by more than 80%. Germany was one of the first EU countries to legislate on industrial emissions. In 1975, the Air Protection Act was passed, which required industrial companies to reduce their emissions. Since then, Germany has repeatedly amended and tightened its industrial emissions regulations. The regulations are now among the strictest in the EU. France has also introduced strict regulations on industrial emissions. The 1996 Air Protection Act requires industrial companies to reduce their emissions of various pollutants, including CO_2, NO_x, sulphur and PM. Sweden is one of the most sustainable countries in the world. It has a long history of implementing sustainable environmental solutions. In 1991, Sweden introduced an environmental law requiring industrial companies to reduce their emissions of various pollutants. EU industrial emissions regulations are an effective tool in protecting the environment and human health. Through strict EU regulations, member countries can reduce industrial emissions and improve air, water, and soil quality.

In some EU countries, there are financial support programs for residents who replace old stoves or boilers with more efficient, environmentally friendly models. Modern stoves and boilers tend to be more efficient and produce less pollution, and they are a significant contributor to exceeding air pollution standards during the winter. In some EU countries, there are financial support programs for residents who replace old stoves or boilers with more efficient, environmentally friendly models. Modern stoves and boilers are usually more efficient and produce less pollution. The "Clean Air" program in Poland offers grants and loans for replacing old coal stoves with new, environmentally friendly heat sources. The program is available to people whose income does not exceed 100% of the average salary in Poland. In France, a program called "Ma Prime Renov" offers subsidies for replacing old stoves with new, environmentally friendly models. The program is available to anyone replacing a stove in their house. Germany is offering the "Bundesförderung für effiziente Gebäude" program to subsidize the replacement of old stoves with new, environmentally friendly models. The program is available to anyone who is replacing a stove in the house where they live. Furnace and boiler replacement programs are an effective way to reduce air pollution. Studies show that replacing old stoves with new ones reduces dust and harmful gas emissions by about 50%.

Another essential element in reducing air pollution is measures to promote changes in lifestyles and consumption. Financial incentives for residents to replace old, less efficient appliances with greener models can help reduce household emissions. Awareness campaigns promoting public transportation, cycling, and car-sharing can change residents' habits and reduce particulate emissions. Lifestyle and consumption changes can significantly contribute to reducing air pollution. For example, reducing energy and fossil fuel consumption can help reduce air pollution emissions from transportation, home heating, and energy production. Choosing environmentally friendly products can also help reduce air pollutant emissions from product manufacturing and disposal.

The EU is taking several actions to promote changes in lifestyles and consumption. These activities include information campaigns. The EU conducts information campaigns to make people aware of the impact of air pollution on health and well-being. These campaigns encourage people to take measures to reduce their impact on air pollution, such as using public transportation, saving energy, and choosing environmentally friendly products. It also implements sustainable mobility initiatives. The EU promotes sustainable mobility through information campaigns, transportation planning initiatives, and financial incentive programs. For example, the EU promotes the use of public transportation and bicycles through the European Sustainable Mobility Week campaign. Complementing the information programs are financial incentive programs for taking action to reduce air pollution. For example, the EU offers subsidies for purchasing EVs and installing solar panels. Through these measures, the EU is helping member states promote a change in lifestyle and consumption, which can significantly contribute to reducing air pollution.

Last, but particularly important, is the joint action of countries. It is unique that such a large group of EU countries have declared cooperation at the international level to solve the air pollution problem. Sharing knowledge, experience, and technology allows effective action to improve air quality. It covers many different aspects, including working on common air quality standards. The EU has developed several air quality directives that set binding emission limits for member states. These directives include the Outdoor Air Quality and Cleaner Air for Europe Directive, the Industrial Emissions Directive and the National Emissions Ceilings Directive (Chapter 2). In addition, it supports research projects aimed at developing new technologies and solutions to reduce air pollution. These projects are funded under the LIFE program and the Horizon Europe program. These are complemented by promoting action to reduce pollution through information campaigns, sustainable mobility initiatives, and financial incentive programs. For example, the EU is promoting the use of public transportation and bicycles through its "European Sustainable Mobility Week" campaign.

In addition to these three main aspects, EU cooperation on air pollution also includes exchanging information and best practices. The EU facilitates the exchange of information and best practices among member states on air pollution. For example, the EU operates the European Environment Agency (EEA), which provides member states with information and scientific support on air pollution. The EU also cooperates with other countries and international organizations to reduce air pollution. For example, the EU is a party to the Convention on Long-Range Transboundary Air Pollution (CLRTAP). By cooperating on air pollution, the EU is helping member states improve air quality and protect the health and well-being of its citizens.

These examples show that EU countries have taken a variety of actions to reduce particulate air pollution. These measures often combine regulations, infrastructure investments, and incentive programs for residents and businesses to improve air quality effectively. Nevertheless, the most important thing is public awareness, which involves understanding the threat of air pollution.

Implementing air quality legislation has yielded valuable lessons that can inform future policy-making efforts. One key lesson is the importance of stakeholder engagement and collaboration in developing and implementing regulations. By involving diverse stakeholders, including industry, government, academia, and civil society, policymakers can build consensus, enhance transparency, and improve the effectiveness of regulatory measures. Furthermore, adopting a comprehensive approach integrating air quality considerations into broader sustainability and public health agendas can facilitate synergies and maximize co-benefits.

The conclusion is that countries can use a variety of practices and strategies to reduce air pollution. Strict regulation, investment in infrastructure, promoting lifestyle changes, and international cooperation are crucial elements of effective policies to improve air quality and protect public health. These actions should be taken with determination and commitment to meet the challenge of air pollution in the 21st century.

4.4 Summary

In conclusion, implementing air quality legislation at the national level has yielded both successes and challenges. By critically examining these experiences and lessons learned, policymakers can better understand the factors driving effective air quality governance and identify strategies to overcome barriers to implementation. Moving forward, it is essential to build on past achievements, leverage emerging technologies and scientific insights, and foster international cooperation to effectively address the complex and interconnected challenges of air pollution. Countries can achieve sustainable, equitable, and healthy air for all through concerted action and shared commitment.

Early action is essential for preventing air pollution. Waiting until air quality problems are severe to act makes solving them more difficult and expensive. For example, it is much more complex and expensive to retrofit a coal-fired power plant with pollution controls than to build a new power plant that is cleaner from the start.

A comprehensive approach is needed to address air pollution. Air pollution comes from various sources, so it is essential to address all sources of pollution to improve air quality. This includes cars, trucks, power plants, industrial facilities, and agriculture.

Public engagement is crucial for success. People are more likely to support policies that improve air quality if they understand the problem and believe they will be effective. Public engagement is also essential for ensuring that policies are fair and that they do not unfairly burden any one group of people.

Economic incentives can be effective in reducing air pollution. Economic incentives, such as taxes on polluting activities or subsidies for cleaner technologies, can be a cost-effective way to reduce air pollution.

Technology is an integral part of the solution. New technologies, such as cleaner engines, more efficient power plants, and better air pollution control devices, can significantly reduce air pollution.

International cooperation is essential. Air pollution does not respect borders, so it is important to work with other countries to reduce it. This includes sharing information about best practices, developing international standards, and funding clean energy projects.

In addition to these general lessons, some specific lessons have been learned from implementing air quality legislation in different countries. For example, one lesson that has been learned is that it is essential to have a robust monitoring system in place to track air quality and measure progress. Another lesson is that it is essential to set clear and ambitious goals and targets for air quality improvement.

Implementing air quality legislation is an ongoing process, and there will continue to be challenges and learning opportunities in the years to come. However, the lessons learned so far can help us develop more effective and lasting solutions to air pollution problems.

Reference list

Abdalla, A. N., Nazir, M. S., Tao, H., Cao, S., Ji, R., Jiang, M., & Yao, L. (2021). Integration of energy storage system and renewable energy sources based on artificial intelligence: An overview. *Journal of Energy Storage*, *40*, 102811. https://doi.org/10.1016/j.est.2021.102811

Arnell, N. W., Lowe, J., Brown, S., Gosling, S., Gottschalk, P., Hinkel, J., Lloyd-Hughes, B., Nicholls, R., Osborn, T., & Osborne, T. M. (2013). A global assessment of the effects of climate policy on the impacts of climate change. *Nature Climate Change*, *3*(5), 512–519.

Barwick, P. J., Li, S., Rao, D., & Zahur, N. B. (2024). The healthcare cost of air pollution: Evidence from the world's largest payment network. *Review of Economics and Statistics*, 1–52.

Blakers, A., Stocks, M., Lu, B., & Cheng, C. (2021). A review of pumped hydro energy storage. *Progress in Energy*, *3*(2), 022003. https://doi.org/10.1088/2516-1083/abeb5b

Boogaard, H., Walker, K., & Cohen, A. J. (2019). Air pollution: The emergence of a major global health risk factor. *International Health*, *11*(6), 417–421.

Brunekreef, B., & Holgate, S. T. (2002). Air pollution and health. *The Lancet*, *360*(9341), 1233–1242. https://doi.org/10.1016/S0140-6736(02)11274-8

Chen, M., Sinha, A., Hu, K., & Shah, M. I. (2021). Impact of technological innovation on energy efficiency in industry 4.0 era: Moderation of shadow economy in sustainable development. *Technological Forecasting and Social Change*, *164*, 120521. https://doi.org/10.1016/j.techfore.2020.120521

Costa, M., Buono, A., Caputo, C., Carotenuto, A., Cirillo, D., Costagliola, M. A., Di Blasio, G., La Villetta, M., Macaluso, A., Martoriello, G., Massarotti, N., Mauro, A., Migliaccio, M., Mulone, V., Murena, F., Piazzullo, D., Prati, M. V., Rocco, V., Stasi, A.,. . . De Vita, A. (2020). The "INNOVARE" project: Innovative plants for distributed poly-generation by residual biomass. *Energies*, *13*(15), 4020. https://doi.org/10.3390/en13154020

Elia, A., Kamidelivand, M., Rogan, F., & Ó Gallachóir, B. (2021). Impacts of innovation on renewable energy technology cost reductions. *Renewable and Sustainable Energy Reviews, 138*, 110488. https://doi.org/10.1016/j.rser.2020.110488

European Automobile Manufacturers Association. (2024, May 7). *Interactive map – Correlation between electric car sales and charging point availability (2023 data)*. ACEA – European Automobile Manufacturers' Association. https://www.acea.auto/figure/interactive-map-correlation-between-electric-car-sales-and-charging-point-availability-2023-data/

European Court of Auditors. (2021). *Infrastruktura ładowania pojazdów elektrycznych: Mimo rosnącej liczby stacji ładowania podróżowanie po UE jest skomplikowane ze względu na ich nierównomierne rozmieszczenie*. Publications Office. https://data.europa.eu/doi/10.2865/909245

European Environment Agency. (2023a). *ETC HE Report 2023/7: Health risk assessment of air pollution: Assessing the environmental burden of disease in Europe in 2021*. Eionet Portal. https://www.eionet.europa.eu/etcs/etc-he/products/etc-he-products/etc-he-reports/etc-he-report-2023-7-health-risk-assessment-of-air-pollution-assessing-the-environmental-burden-of-disease-in-europe-in-2021

European Environment Agency. (2023b, November 24). *Premature deaths due to exposure to fine particulate matter in Europe*. https://www.eea.europa.eu/en/analysis/indicators/health-impacts-of-exposure-to

European Parliament and the Council of the European Union. (2023). *Directive – EU – 2023/2413 – EN – Renewable energy directive – EUR-Lex*. https://eur-lex.europa.eu/eli/dir/2023/2413/oj

Eurostat. (2021). *Net greenhouse gas emissions*. https://ec.europa.eu/eurostat/databrowser/view/sdg_13_10/default/table?lang=en&category=sdg.sdg_13

Eurostat. (2022). *Share of renewable energy in gross final energy consumption*. https://ec.europa.eu/eurostat/databrowser/view/SDG_07_40/default/table?lang=en

Eurostat. (2024a). *Climate related economic losses by type of event*. https://ec.europa.eu/eurostat/databrowser/product/page/CLI_IAD_LOSS

Eurostat. (2024b). *Electricity production capacities for renewables and wastes*. https://ec.europa.eu/eurostat/databrowser/product/page/NRG_INF_EPCRW

Eurostat. (2024c). *Heat pumps – Technical characteristics by technologies*. https://ec.europa.eu/eurostat/databrowser/view/NRG_INF_HPTC/default/table

Eurostat. (2024d). *Liquid biofuels production capacities*. https://ec.europa.eu/eurostat/databrowser/product/page/NRG_INF_LBPC

Eurostat. (2024e). *Share of new zero-emission vehicles in all new vehicles of the same type, by type of vehicle and type of motor energy*. https://ec.europa.eu/eurostat/databrowser/view/ROAD_EQR_ZEVPC/default/table

Eurostat. (2024f). Solar thermal collectors' surface. *Statistics*. https://ec.europa.eu/eurostat/databrowser/product/page/nrg_inf_stcs$defaultview

Forzieri, G., Bianchi, A., Silva, F. B. E., Marin Herrera, M. A., Leblois, A., Lavalle, C., Aerts, J. C. J. H., & Feyen, L. (2018). Escalating impacts of climate extremes on critical infrastructures in Europe. *Global Environmental Change, 48*, 97–107. https://doi.org/10.1016/j.gloenvcha.2017.11.007

Government of the Grand Duchy of Luxembourg. (2024, January 25). *Public transport.* http://luxembourg.public.lu/en/living/mobility/public-transport.html

Katsouyanni, K. (2003). Ambient air pollution and health. *British Medical Bulletin, 68*(1), 143–156.

Kostecka-Jurczyk, D., & Marak, K. (2024). Spółdzielnie energetyczne i klastry energii jako formy energetyki obywatelskiej w Polsce. *Studia Prawnoustrojowe, 63.* https://doi.org/10.31648/sp.9596

Luan, C., Sun, X., & Wang, Y. (2021). Driving forces of solar energy technology innovation and evolution. *Journal of Cleaner Production, 287*, 125019. https://doi.org/10.1016/j.jclepro.2020.125019

Miao, C., Fang, D., Sun, L., Luo, Q., & Yu, Q. (2018). Driving effect of technology innovation on energy utilization efficiency in strategic emerging industries. *Journal of Cleaner Production, 170*, 1177–1184. https://doi.org/10.1016/j.jclepro.2017.09.225

Odam, N., & De Vries, F. P. (2020). Innovation modelling and multi-factor learning in wind energy technology. *Energy Economics, 85*, 104594. https://doi.org/10.1016/j.eneco.2019.104594

Oryani, B., Koo, Y., Rezania, S., & Shafiee, A. (2021). Barriers to renewable energy technologies penetration: Perspective in Iran. *Renewable Energy, 174*, 971–983.

Pasqualetti, M. J. (2011). Social barriers to renewable energy landscapes. *Geographical Review, 101*(2), 201–223.

Piontek, F., Müller, C., Pugh, T. A., Clark, D. B., Deryng, D., Elliott, J., Colón González, F. de J., Flörke, M., Folberth, C., & Franssen, W. (2014). Multisectoral climate impact hotspots in a warming world. *Proceedings of the National Academy of Sciences, 111*(9), 3233–3238.

Pyk, A. (2023). Mikrosieci jako wzorcowe rozwiązania zarządzające odnawialnymi zasobami energii. *Zeszyty Naukowe Akademii Górnośląskiej, 6.*

Schwela, D. (2000). Air pollution and health in urban areas. *Reviews on Environmental Health, 15*(1–2), 13–42.

Sen, S., & Ganguly, S. (2017). Opportunities, barriers and issues with renewable energy development–A discussion. *Renewable and Sustainable Energy Reviews, 69*, 1170–1181.

Smart City Sweden. (2024). *Swedish national environmental quality objectives: Clean air.* Smart City Sweden. https://smartcitysweden.com/focus-areas/climate-environment/air-quality/

Visit Sweden. (2024). *Sweden's best cycling routes.* https://visitsweden.com/what-to-do/nature-outdoors/biking/swedens-best-cycling-routes/

Volvo. (2024). *Zrównoważone systemy transportowe.* https://www.volvogroup.com/pl/sustainability/environmental-resources-efficiency/sustainable-transport-system.html

World Health Organization. (2018). *Burden of disease from the joint effects of household and ambient air pollution for 2016.* https://cdn.who.int/media/docs/default-source/air-quality-database/aqd-2018/ap_joint_effect_bod_results_may2018.pdf

Appendix A.1

CO_2 emissions – trends

Country	p-value	Estimate	Trend
Austria	0.5838		Lack
Belgium	8.765e-11	−0.60116	Decreasing
Bulgaria	4.443e-07	−1.2209	Decreasing
Croatia	0.9773		Lack
Cyprus	0.00155	5.854	Increasing
Denmark	5.068e-14	−0.66776	Decreasing
Estonia	0.003934	−1.5351	Decreasing
Finland	2.44e-05	−0.6530	Decreasing
France	1.52e-08	−0.1890	Decreasing
Germany	2.063e-15	−9.919e-02	Decreasing
Greece	0.002795	−0.27525	Decreasing
Hungary	3.732e-11	−1.180	Decreasing
Ireland	0.8397		Lack
Italy	7.83e-06	−0.10679	Decreasing
Latvia	8.254e-05	−3.7609	Decreasing
Lithuania	0.006051	−2.489	Decreasing
Luxembourg	0.2498		Lack
Malta	2.775e-05	−12.939	Decreasing
The Netherlands	1.781e-05	−0.5843	Decreasing
Poland	0.0002574	−0.27847	Decreasing
Portugal	0.01831	−0.4649	Decreasing
Romania	5.398e-11	−0.4526	Decreasing
Slovakia	1.003e-14	−1.8715	Decreasing
Slovenia	0.05779		Lack
Spain	0.3305		Lack
Sweden	2.995e-15	−1.10858	Decreasing

PM$_{10}$ – *trends*

Country	p-value	Estimate	Trend
Austria	2.2e-16	-1.398e-03	Decreasing
Belgium	2.899e-15	-6.734e-04	Decreasing
Bulgaria	3.538e-07	-6.128e-04	Decreasing
Croatia	8.186e-08	-1.079e-03	Decreasing
Cyprus	3.891e-11	-1.115e-02	Decreasing
Denmark	4.972e-07	-1.605e-03	Decreasing
Estonia	0.001091	-1.561e-03	Decreasing
Finland	5.029e-15	-1.472e-03	Decreasing
France	5.831e-16	-9.769e-05	Decreasing
Germany	2.2e-16	-2.629e-04	Decreasing
Greece	5.148e-12	-4.519e-04	Decreasing
Hungary	0.7781		Lack
Ireland	3.529e-12	-2.489e-03	Decreasing
Italy	0.0009437	-1.763e-04	Decreasing
Latvia	9.335e-10	-1.283e-03	Decreasing
Lithuania	0.6909		Lack
Luxembourg	2.252e-13	-1.190e-02	Decreasing
Malta	1.794e-08	-0.03385	Decreasing
The Netherlands	2.2e-16	-9.924e-04	Decreasing
Poland	0.7275		Lack
Portugal	2.191e-11	-9.226e-04	Decreasing
Romania	0.3299		Lack
Slovakia	3.683e-09	-7.524e-04	Decreasing
Slovenia	1.851e-06	-2.841e-03	Decreasing
Spain	1.205e-09	-3.370e-04	Decreasing
Sweden	2.2e-16	-1.090e-03	Decreasing
EU	1.688e-14	-2.118e-05	Decreasing

PM$_{2.5}$ – *trends*

Country	p-value	Estimate	Trend
Austria	2.2e-16	-1.701e-03	Decreasing
Belgium	2.2e-16	-8.363e-04	Decreasing
Bulgaria	0.0001792	-1.348e-03	Decreasing
Croatia	8.186e-08	-1.079e-03	Decreasing
Cyprus	3.891e-11	-1.115e-02	Decreasing
Denmark	4.972e-07	-1.605e-03	Decreasing
Estonia	0.001091	-1.561e-03	Decreasing
Finland	5.029e-15	-1.472e-03	Decreasing
France	5.831e-16	-9.769e-05	Decreasing
Germany	2.2e-16	-2.629e-04	Decreasing
Greece	5.148e-12	-4.519e-04	Decreasing
Hungary	0.7781		Lack
Ireland	3.529e-12	-2.489e-03	Decreasing

(Continued)

PM$_{2.5}$ – *trends* (Continued)

Country	p-value	Estimate	Trend
Italy	0.0009437	−1.763e-04	Decreasing
Latvia	9.335e-10	−1.283e-03	Decreasing
Lithuania	0.6909		Lack
Luxembourg	2.252e-13	−1.190e-02	Decreasing
Malta	1.794e-08	−0.03385	Decreasing
The Netherlands	2.2e-16	−9.924e-04	Decreasing
Poland	0.7275		Lack
Portugal	2.191e-11	−9.226e-04	Decreasing
Romania	0.3299		Lack
Slovakia	3.683e-09	−7.524e-04	Decreasing
Slovenia	1.851e-06	−2.841e-03	Decreasing
Spain	1.205e-09	−3.370e-04	Decreasing
Sweden	2.2e-16	−1.090e-03	Decreasing
EU	3.933e-14	−3.069e-05	Decreasing

Index

For Product Safety Concerns and Information please contact our EU
representative GPSR@taylorandfrancis.com
Taylor & Francis Verlag GmbH, Kaufingerstraße 24, 80331 München, Germany